RELATIONSHIPS

Connecting the Knots in the Threads of Life

by Skip Heitzig

CONNECTION COMMUNICATIONS

4001 Osuna Road Northeast • Albuquerque, NM 87109 USA • 1-800-922-1888

CONNECTION COMMUNICATIONS 1997

Unless otherwise indicated, Scripture quotations used in this
book are from the New King James Version of the Bible.
Copyright ©1979, 1980, 1982
by Thomas Nelson Publishers, Inc.

ISBN 1-886324-06-9

Published by CONNECTION PUBLISHING
Cover Design by Stephen T. Eames
Edited by Laura Z. Sowers
Printed in USA

Forward

We were created by God to crave and to enjoy relationships. This craving was designed by God to draw us into a meaningful relationship with Him and with others.

Strong, lasting relationships are often difficult to develop. In this book, Skip lays out sound Biblical principles to help you develop good, healthy relationships. You will find valuable insights to help you make the most of every relationship. In the book of Romans, Paul tells us that no one lives unto himself. Loneliness can be a sort of hell; God recognized this when He declared, "It is not good that man should be alone." Skip gives practical advice concerning loneliness and how to open the door to meaningful relationships.

The rules for dating are especially helpful for those who are looking for God's chosen partner for their lives. Those who have found that one and have committed before God to be faithful until-death-do-you-part will find the chapter on marriage very helpful.

For those who find themselves in the role of single parents, the problems of relationships can sometimes be especially difficult—you also will find helpful spiritual guidance in the chapter devoted to these distinctive problems.

The bottom line is this: Good relationships make for a good life; good relationships don't "just happen," they are developed by following solid biblical principles.

These principles have been searched out and presented in an interesting and practical way in this book.

—Chuck Smith

Preface

If life was boiled down to its essence, I believe the most valued common element would be our relationships. Solomon looked at relationships as a source of support, comfort, and strength. Like a rope comprised of individual cords, our relationship-threads weave the fabric of our lives:

> *Two are better than one, because they have a good reward for their labor. For if they fall, one will lift up his companion. But woe to him who is alone when he falls, for he has no one to help him up. Again, if two lie down together, they will keep warm; but how can one be warm alone? Though one may be overpowered by another, two can withstand him. And a three-fold cord is not quickly broken. (Eccles. 4:9-12)*

Unfortunately, sometimes we don't realize the importance of our relationships until a crisis occurs, such as a debilitating disease or, worse, the death of a loved one. Then we lament, "I should have spent more time with her," or "I wish we had been able to talk openly with each other." Our frantic pace can blind us to the reality that true happiness is not found by attaining those goals but is the by-product of fulfilling relationships.

All relationships are not created equal. Our relationships with God and our families provide the basic cords that keep us tethered to bearings and values. When our relationships are woven together biblically, life is rewarding and fulfilling. We shouldn't be surprised to discover that when we operate according to our Manufacturer's specifications and directions, we will perform at our peak.

The main focus of this book, therefore, is on the basic human relationship which, from the beginning, God regarded as primary: marriage. He looked upon Adam and remarked, "It is not good that man should be alone. I will make a helper comparable to him." One man and one woman form the fundamental relationship of society—the bedrock of all other relationships. It is also the one which draws the most fire from supporters of humanism and pluralism.

The lines of right and wrong, which were once clearly defined and understood, have now become blurred. Sex before marriage is considered normal. Divorce seems to be the inevitable option when a marriage encounters trouble. In Western civilization, the homosexual lifestyle has been dignified to the extent that it is no longer even questioned.

In pastoring a congregation of more than ten thousand, I am acutely aware that people have many questions about their relationships. In a church of this size, however, it is difficult to know the specific concerns, problems, and the confusing "hot potato" issues Christians face and want to understand from the biblical perspective.

With this in mind, I decided to conduct a poll asking the congregation to tell me what was heavy on their minds and hearts. In polling them, I threw out my net expecting a varied, eclectic response, but that was not what I found when I drew the net back in. There were several questions about the "end times" and a few other difficult theological concepts. But the overwhelming thirst was for biblical answers and guidance in relationships. While I expected some interest in this, I was unprepared for the volume of questions relating to how to have meaningful, successful relationships. Some of the predominant concerns were:

- Why do I still feel lonely even though I'm married?
- Can I have a fulfilled life as a single person?
- What does the Bible say about dating?
- What is the secret of a healthy, fulfilling marriage?
- What do you do if you're married to an unbeliever?
- My relationships are already fractured; now what?

This book is a response to these and other questions. However, this volume is necessarily limited in its scope and far from being a comprehensive treatise on all the varied and complex relational threads we weave through life. Much more could be said about parent/child relationships, friendships, professional relationships, and so on, but I have seen how liberating God's principles can be when applied by those who sincerely seek and obey them.

It is my hope that God uses this information to enrich your life, and as you follow His guidelines, your relationships will be enjoyed as God intended.

—*Skip Heitzig*

Table of Contents

Chapter One

A Problem Observed:
The Nagging Sting of Loneliness

The Faces of Loneliness

In sorting through the numerous responses to my poll, I found many unspoken, heartfelt sentiments tucked between the written lines. Beneath the surface of words and spiritual-sounding questions, I discovered an undercurrent of pain and alienation. Many Christians have unrealistic expectations of themselves, of other people, and of God. The result can be the very real problem of *loneliness*.

Loneliness wears many faces. We would expect to find it in the eyes of the prison inmate, hear it in the voice of the divorced parent, or see it in the hopeless expression of the elderly in a nursing home. But loneliness is far more prevalent than this. People we may never suspect can be aching and forlorn although they appear to be spiritual and "together." Some of the loneliest people may even be sitting next to us in church. Beneath the smiles and small talk, the praising and prayers, there is suffering going on in the Body of Christ—the nagging sting of loneliness. Let me share a letter I recently received:

I write this to you hurting so bad, I even cry myself to sleep, and I'm tired of doing that. I still pray every day that I could make it through another day. It's getting ever so hard for me to live. Am I doing something wrong? I don't understand. It's so hard to make friends these days, even with Christians. I tried. Sometimes maybe I don't understand what it is to be a true Christian. I thought we were supposed to be images of Christ. You see people who attend church daily, weekly, or in prayer services, born-again Christians, but you want and need to talk to somebody, to be a friend. They do it out of sympathy or, sometimes, turn their cheek in a very nice manner. What happened to doing things for love—loving you just the way you are? You need to fit into their category as a good person. Christians can be judgmental without realizing that Christians are sad too. And, just because you are a born-again Christian doesn't mean everything is okay.

In truth, many people could echo those attitudes because loneliness isn't confined to the single lifestyle or to the "Lonely Hearts Club." Even in marriages, loneliness shows its somber face. Sometimes a spouse is consumed by work and neglects his mate and family. For others, years of marriage, love, and compassion have been replaced by aloof ambivalence. Still others are coping with the loneliness unique to the Christian believer married to an unbeliever, as the following letter describes:

How do I, as a woman, deal with a spouse who is not interested in God, Christianity, or church? How do I handle a home life without God and the Christian faith? How do I beat loneliness? People not wanting me? How do I show Christianity when I feel so sad and so lonely?

2

Marriage and family bring incredible responsibilities. When only one of the partners bears the majority of the load, the result can be alienation and resentment.

Solomon wrote about the need for friendships and warned of the famine of isolation when he said, "...woe to him who is alone when he falls, for he has no one to help him up" (Eccles. 4:10).

Even in the Bible

Loneliness is nothing new. Long before these letters were sent to me, loneliness was a reality in the lives of God's people. Even those righteous and faithful pioneers of faith had their bouts with it. In fact, because the psalms often reflect the feelings in our own hearts, Christians throughout the centuries have loved reading them. The following words are from a lonely man pouring out his heart to God:

Turn to me and be gracious to me, for I am lonely and afflicted. The troubles of my heart have multiplied; free me from my anguish. (Ps. 25:16-17, NIV)

This is not the cry of an unbeliever wallowing in aimlessness but the honest prayer of David, Israel's beloved psalmist and King, revealing his heartache to God. On another occasion the psalmist prayed:

Hear my prayer, O Lord, and let my cry come to You.
Do not hide Your face from me in the day of my trouble;
Incline Your ear to me;
In the day that I call, answer me speedily.
For my days are consumed like smoke,
And my bones are burned like a hearth.
My heart is stricken and withered like grass,
So that I forget to eat my bread.
Because of the sound of my groaning
My bones cling to my skin.

I am like a pelican of the wilderness;
I am like an owl of the desert.
I lie awake,
And am like a sparrow alone on the housetop.
(Ps. 102:1-7)

Did you catch those descriptions? "My heart is stricken...my groaning...I lie awake." Does this sound like an excerpt from your journal? This guy was in anguished prayer during a very lonely episode in his life. And he wasn't the only one. People like Elijah, Jeremiah, and Paul rank among those who experienced similar spells. The great Apostle Paul, a spiritual giant and pioneer of the gospel, went through lonely valleys. Toward the end of his life, he divulged to Timothy, "At my first defense no one stood with me, but all forsook me. May it not be charged against them." However, he was quick to add, "But the Lord stood with me and strengthened me…." (2 Tim. 4:16-17).

What Loneliness Is—and What It Isn't

Webster instructs us that loneliness is "the state of being without company; to be cut off from others, not frequented by human beings." Good try, Webster, but I don't think that quite cuts it. There are some experiences that are hard to *define* but easy to *feel*. Have you ever tried to define being in love? Can you quickly explain the feeling of anger or verbalize the disappointment of trying to achieve a goal—and failing? Tough, isn't it? But I would bet that you could close your eyes and, with a little concentration, recall how those situations *feel*. So it is with loneliness. It's easier to understand how loneliness feels than to define it.

Loneliness Is Not Seclusion

Being alone does not necessarily equal loneliness. The absence of people is sometimes necessary and even desirable. All of us need a certain amount of space and privacy. Being alone allows our inner man to connect with God. Jesus often

4

spent time alone with the Father, and we should also seek out times of solitude and communion with God. Getting away from it all for awhile is often the best thing we can do.

Loneliness Is...

Loneliness is feeling isolated even when surrounded by crowds of people. The famous scientist, Albert Einstein, once commented, "It's strange to be known so universally and yet be so lonely." Loneliness is a feeling of being unwanted, abandoned, and hopeless. The best definition I've come across is from Warren Wiersbe, former pastor of the famed Moody Memorial Church in Chicago, who said, "Loneliness is the malnutrition of the soul that comes from living on substitutes." That hits the nail on the head, doesn't it? When we replace substance with substitutes; when we reach for lust rather than love, money rather than true spiritual wealth, power rather than peace, the result will always be the same—loneliness and alienation. An esteemed Jewish rabbi from the twelfth century once wrote, "There is none more lonely than the man who loves only himself."

Not long ago, I attended a lecture on transcendental meditation, an Eastern cult based on Hinduism, thinly disguised in scientific, philosophical garb. I sat in the back of the room, ready and waiting. The speakers were offering inner peace for $600 a whack! Following payment of this fee, the new convert would repeat an introductory prayer in Sanskrit and be given a monosyllabic "mantra" to chant while practicing relaxation techniques.

When the floor was opened for questions, I raised my hand and stood up. "Excuse me," I said. "You've told us this evening that transcendental meditation has nothing to do with religion—it's just a proven, scientific method."

They nodded their agreement.

"Are you sure," I continued, "this has nothing to do with religion?"

"Absolutely," they said.

"Well, what about the introductory passage that everyone is required to read and recite in order to be taught the technique? And what about the little word that no one understands? Why isn't it in English?"

They replied, "We believe it preserves the antiquity of the technique and...."

I interrupted and said, "I just happen to have with me the English translation of this introductory rite. Would you mind if I read it?"

Before they could say no, I began reading. It was filled with prayers offered to Hindu deities. I wanted to reveal that this religious cult was masking its true identity. They were blatantly religious, yet they tried to come off as scientific in order to lend credibility to their scheme.

I continued to press the point. "I feel you owe these people the truth about what they are paying $600 for. They need to know they are buying into a system of Eastern religious mysticism. It is not scientific. It's fake." I concluded by telling them that Jesus Christ offers peace, satisfaction, and an abundant life for free.

Surprisingly, I was not admonished by the leadership of this meeting but by the people in the audience. One fellow turned around and said, "Would you shut up!" It stunned me that this person was in effect saying, "Would you please let me be deceived and allow me to be duped! Quit telling me the truth—I want to pay $600 to purchase this lie—this substitute for peace and satisfaction."

There are many people who settle for substitutes rather than the real peace and intimacy of a relationship with God. Dr. Paul Morentz, Lutheran pastor and psychiatrist, says, "Loneliness is still mankind's greatest problem. And it stems from...man's self-imposed loneliness and isolation from God back in the Garden of Eden."

Why Are We Lonely?

In our society, mobility is one of many factors which separates us from one another and breeds loneliness. Ours is a generation of relocation. At any given moment, up to one-fifth of our neighbors are pulling up roots and settling down somewhere else. The result is many casual contacts and very few long-term, meaningful relationships. Chances are that at best, we know only a handful of the people around us, and many of those relationships are superficial.

Another reason for our loneliness is that we're afraid of each other. We are appalled when we read the newspaper and view crime reports on television. We have dead bolts and chains on our doors; we have guns in our homes, and our houses are wired with alarms.

Recently, I spoke to a woman in a southern city who confessed she was afraid to use the automated teller machine at any bank—even in broad daylight! Not long ago, thirty people in our community were held at gunpoint—*in their church!*

Some people are hesitant to form close ties with other people because they fear if they let down their guard and take the risk, they'll get hurt. Anyone who has been betrayed or taken advantage of by a friend can relate. We react to our hurt by building a wall around ourselves, saying, "I've tried to get close and I got burned—I won't let it happen again." Whenever walls, rather than bridges, are erected, the outcome will be loneliness.

The most significant cause for this pervasive malady, however, is spiritual. Sin separates us from the very God who loves us and desires to genuinely satisfy our lives with His fellowship. One psychiatrist was asked, "What is the predominate problem among the people who come to you for help?" He responded, "Loneliness. In fact, when you get down to it, it is loneliness for God!" Sin separates us from

God and from each other.

These are obvious causes of loneliness which generally apply to society. Oddly, Christians can experience a peculiar loneliness for reasons directly related to their beliefs. We don't expect to find detached and isolated believers in the midst of a Christian fellowship, but they are there, silently suffering in the "slough of despond." Why?

Christian Myths: Lies That Unbind

In my pastoring, I talk with people every day. I've noticed several common, yet unbiblical, misconceptions that tend to heap more disappointment on already broken spirits. Wrong thinking and unrealistic expectations of the Christian life create a sense of isolation. It's important that we confront these myths so we can live realistically and in confidence.

Myth #1: The "Fairy Tale" Complex

We all love stories that end, "And they lived happily ever after." Some expect the same outcome when they choose to follow Christ. After all, if Disney could pull it off, why can't God? Trials should cease, tribulations become past tense, and all Christians live happily ever after. Right? Wrong.

This tendency to sugar-coat the Christian life creates false expectations which can be especially damaging to the unbeliever and the new believer. If we tell them, "Just accept Jesus and everything will be great," guess what? When the trials of life continue, they will feel misled and disappointed. While a relationship with Jesus means an abundant life, it does not mean an *easy* life. Too many offer a glitzy, maintenance-free Jesus with no unpleasant aftertaste.

All this is symptomatic of our quick fix, bumpersticker world. Ours is a society of slogans: "Christians aren't perfect, they're just forgiven," "Praise the Lord," "Let go and let God," and so on. While there are some wonderful truths to these axioms, they foster the notion that the Christian life is a snap, and if we happen to hit some rugged spots along the way, just "let go," and God will fix everything.

Being a Christian doesn't mean we can write checks when there's no money in the bank or drive a car without putting gasoline in the tank. Although I've heard and observed God's supernatural power on many occasions, we're still subject to the demands and stresses of the real world. To expect otherwise is to walk the path of eventual disappointment. Why would Christ have urged us to count the cost in following Him unless He wanted us to have realistic expectations of the challenges before us? He knew that living as a believer sometimes means picking up the sword and trudging into battle.

One day, when Jesus returns, we *will* live happily ever after. The time is coming when there will be no pain, no financial frustrations, no heartache of any kind. But that time is not yet here. Paul reminded the persecuted believers in Rome of this when he said, "For I consider that the *sufferings of this present time* are not worthy to be compared with the glory which shall be revealed in us" (Rom. 8:18, emphasis mine). Now that's balance.

In C.S. Lewis' excellent book, *The Screwtape Letters,* we are privy to a conversation between two demons. One counsels the other to take advantage of the new Christian a few weeks after he comes to the Lord. When the glow fades, a period of disappointment can set in. At this point, the demon instructs, the new believer is confronted with the realization that his problems and disappointments were not automatically solved or eliminated by asking Jesus into his heart. The demon was aware that these unrealistic expectations create the perfect climate for Satan to try and snatch the Word from our hearts.

Myth #2: The "Parade Smile" Complex

Along with the myth that Christians shouldn't *have* problems comes the equally destructive myth that we should not *show* our problems. "Put on a happy face," or "Christians shouldn't let their problems show," are a couple of ways we perpetuate this myth. We pridefully believe that in voicing our difficulties and disappointments, we may reveal our spiritual immaturity to other believers. Hogwash!

Paul, one of the most mature Christians we find on the pages of Scripture, had an abundance of trials and tribulations which he openly shared with others.

> *For we do not want you to be ignorant, brethren, of our trouble which came to us in Asia: that we were burdened beyond measure, above strength, so that we despaired even of life. (2 Cor. 1:8)*

Now that's what I call being transparent and vulnerable! The popular misconception today is that a mature Christian has it all together, is impervious to pain, and is always smiling. In truth, our smiles are often a thin veneer covering the problems and worries we are reluctant to show for fear of being judged and rejected. Inside, we hunger to be loved and accepted for who we are—weaknesses, flaws, and all. Church is not just for people who have their acts together (anyway, only Jesus has His act together). It's been well said that the church is not a museum for saints but a hospital for sinners! Being authentic means being willing to reveal our true feelings and admit we are human.

Myth #3: The "Elijah" Complex

One of the most isolating of the Christian myths is the belief that no one else has experienced our particular problem and, therefore, something must be wrong with us. In my ministry and counseling, I have found this is just plain wrong. The vast majority of our problems are experienced by other Christians, too. In 1 Kings 19 we learn that when Elijah was in the wilderness running from Jezebel, he cried out to God, saying, "Oh, God, kill me. I don't want to live anymore. I alone have remembered Your covenant. *I am the only one* left and I am being persecuted. I want to die."

The essence of God's response was, "Get up! Do you think you're the only one with this problem? I've got seven thousand prophets just like you who haven't bowed to Baal and who are equally persecuted. You're not the only one!"

The knowledge that we are not alone in our problems should unite, rather than isolate us. Like Elijah, we often indulge in self-pity and self-righteousness.

Myth #4: The "Consumer" Complex

"Everything will be O.K. if I can just find the right church—one with all the right ingredients: good Bible teaching, inspiring worship, and nice people." Those are the unspoken thoughts of many Christians who set out to "shop" for just the right church. They imagine the grass will be greener but, like the sheep who finally cross to the other side of the fence, they are disappointed to find there are rocks in that soil, too.

No matter how gifted the teacher or how nice the people, simply attending a good church doesn't make problems go away. Consider Judas Iscariot. He spent three years with the Source Himself: Jesus. Judas not only failed to flourish and mature as a Christian, but his blatant sin launched a chain of events that led to Christ's death!

Maturity is not an event, it's a process. We can't flip it on like a light switch or whip it up by simply adding water. We don't suddenly become mature while sitting in church one Sunday.

If we attended a lecture series on marathon running, we would hardly expect to leave that lecture hall and appear at the starting line to run twenty-six miles. We would diligently train and practice for weeks, or months, or years. Although we may have acquired an intellectual understanding of marathon running, that knowledge is of little practical use until it is applied to the actual practice of running. Yet we often come to church and wait to be fed truth and become mature without any additional individual effort. It just won't happen. What is *heard* must be *heeded*. If not, we will simply join the ranks of the ever-dissatisfied. Our church-shopping will become church-hopping and maybe even church-dropping since people continually disappoint us. Is it any wonder that the myth of the perfect church contributes to the problem of loneliness?

Let's Get Real—Let's Get Rooted

The Christian life is a real life, complete with trials, tribulations, times of loneliness, and heartache. However, unlike those living apart from Christ, we have hope. Remember, David said he walked *through* the valley of the shadow of death. He didn't get airlifted out! We are not victorious through these trials because we plastered on a fake smile or held everything inside. We are victorious because Jesus' death has allowed Him to live through us. He's our power source.

Rx for Loneliness: A Faith Lift

What practical steps can we take to assess our condition and improve the lonely areas of our lives? Let's look deeper into the elements of the treatment for loneliness. With the help of an acronym, we find what we need to handle loneliness is a "Faith Lift."

> **F**oundation in Christ
> **A**bide in the Word
> **I**nvolvement with Believers
> **T**ies That Bind—with Many
> **H**eaven Bound/Homeward Bound

Foundation In Christ

If we built a home by haphazardly erecting walls, adding doors and windows, and topping it off with a roof, we might have a house that looked okay, for awhile. But when the first storm buffeted our structure, we would become painfully aware that our lovely looking home couldn't bear up to the stress. At that point, the need for that invisible, but vital, missing foundation, would become painfully obvious. In the same way, we need a solid foundation in Jesus Christ if we are to withstand the storms and sorrows of life.

Jesus used this same image when speaking to His followers. The one who comes to Him and obeys Him is like a man who built his house by digging deep and laying a foundation upon solid bedrock. When the floods and winds battered the house, it stood steady because it had solid underpinnings.

By the way, Jesus said *when* the storm arose, not *if*. Like it or not, lonely and stormy times will come our way. The way to survive those periods is by having our lives built on the foundation of Jesus Christ. The hymnist, Edward Mote, knew Christ is the only security when he wrote:

> My hope is built on nothing less
> Than Jesus' blood and righteousness.
> I dare not trust the sweetest frame,
> But wholly lean on Jesus' name.
> On Christ the Solid Rock I stand;
> All other ground is sinking sand.
> All other ground is sinking sand.

Abide in the Word

Other relationships may fail and leave us lonely but, as Christians, we have a permanent position with Christ. Like all relationships, our life with Christ takes an investment of time if it is to grow. Jesus told us, "If you abide in My word, you are My disciples indeed" (John 8:31).

The key word is *abide* which means "permanence and continuance." Jesus spoke of our relationship to God as comparable to a branch clinging to the trunk of a tree. This "abiding" relationship is one in which the branch literally resides in the trunk of the tree. Nutrients flow from the roots, through the trunk, and out into the branches, ultimately producing fruit. Similarly, our lives should be connected closely, fully, and on a daily basis to Jesus Christ. "Abide in Me," He said, "and I in you." This is the ultimate answer—a life immersed in Christ through consistent prayer and reading the Word of God—the Bible.

John Huss, the fifteenth century martyr who was burned to death for his beliefs, had this in mind when he wrote:

Seek the truth
Listen to the truth
Teach the truth
Love the truth
Abide by the truth
And defend the truth
Unto death.

We have a responsibility to maintain a *consistent* walk with the Lord. If I bought a tree from a nursery, planted it in the front yard, and watered it daily, the tree would steadily grow. However, if I dug it up a week later because I decided it would look better in the back yard, the uprooting would damage the tender new roots, and it would have to start over in the growing process. Then if I failed to water it for several days, the tree would go into shock and I would have to call in the plant paramedics. Consistent nurturing is vital for steady growth.

Similarly, when we serve and abide in God and then

uproot ourselves by turning away from Him, we will find ourselves in spiritual shock. He will always accept us when we return. However, by going back and forth, we stunt our growth by interrupting the consistent nurturing we need. An abiding relationship with Christ forms strong, deep roots that sustain and comfort. We are then able to deal with life's problems and reach our spiritual potential. Consistency is the jewel of a mature Christian.

Involvement with Believers

Have you noticed that many Christians have become aloof these days? They come to church and sit alone. "I'm here," they tell themselves. "I'll listen, and then I'll leave." We have become remote, detached, and independent. The philosophy that "it's just me and God, and we'll go it alone," is just plain unbiblical. We Americans love our independence, but God designed us to be interdependent with Him as our foundation.

Paul likens the church to a living and dynamic body. The Body of Christ should function together with Jesus as the head and the Holy Spirit as the nervous system which conveys Christ's directions to the individual members.

Think about the unity of the various components of our bodies as we perform the simplest functions. When we are hungry, our stomachs begin to rumble, sending a message to the brain that we need food. The brain signals our legs to walk toward the fridge; another message is sent to our hand to open the door, and so on. The result is relief from our hunger. The various parts of our body work together harmoniously to accomplish our needs.

This is the interaction we should strive for with other Christians. How connected are you to the other members of your local church? Are you involved interactively, or is church a spectator sport? Without true Christian fellowship, you're destined to wither into a lonely shell of disillusionment. Someone might object by saying, "I've tried to get close to other people, and I've been deeply hurt. I don't think I can trust anyone again." Trusting is risky, but the alternative is imprisoning.

In a recent television biography, Benedict Arnold was portrayed as a tragic figure. As an officer in the British army, he returned to England only to be shunned and ostracized by other officers. Being cut off and isolated was a far worse punishment than imprisonment for his betrayal.

We need one another. Relationships within the church must be actively sought out and maintained. It is not always easy, but Solomon advised, "A man who has friends must himself be friendly..." (Prov. 18:24).

My wife handed me the following story some time back which gave me fresh perspective on the importance of interactive fellowship:

Dr. Harry F. Harlow loved to stand by the animal cages in his University of Wisconsin Laboratory and watch baby monkeys. Intrigued, he noticed that the monkeys seemed emotionally attached to cloth pads lying in their cages. They caressed the cloths, cuddled next to them, and treated them much as children treated teddy bears. In fact, monkeys raised in cages with cloths on the floor grew huskier and healthier than monkeys in cages with wire-mesh floors. Was the softness and touchability of the cloth an important factor? Harlow constructed an ingenious surrogate mother out of terry cloth with a light bulb behind her to radiate heat. The cloth mother featured a rubber nipple attached to a milk supply from which the babies could feed. They adopted her with great enthusiasm. Why not? She was always comfortingly available and, unlike real mothers, never roughed them up or bit them or pushed them aside. After proving that babies could be trained by an inanimate surrogate mother, Harlow next sought to measure the importance of the mother's soft, touchable characteristics. He put eight baby monkeys in a large cage that contained the terry cloth mother plus a new mother. This one was made entirely out of wire mesh. Harlow's assistants, controlling the milk flow to each mother, taught four of the babies to eat from the terry cloth mother and four from the wire-mesh mother. Each baby could obtain milk only from the mother assigned to it. A startling trend developed immediately. All eight babies spent their waking moments, sixteen to eighteen hours a day, huddled next to the terry cloth mother. They hugged her, patted her, perched on her. The monkeys assigned to the wire-mesh mother went to her only for feeding, then hurried back to the comfort and protection of the terry cloth mother. When frightened, all eight sought comfort by climbing onto the terry cloth mother. Harlow said, "We were not surprised that the contact comfort was an important basic affection or love variable, but we did not expect it to so completely overshadow the variable of nursing. Indeed, the disparity is so great as to suggest that the primary function of nursing is that of insuring frequent and intimate body contact of the infant with the mother." He concluded, "Certainly man cannot live by milk alone."

In other experiments, some baby monkeys were raised in cages with only a wire-mesh mother. They, too, approached her only for feeding, and many of these babies did not survive. Those who did survive reacted to stress by cowering in a corner, screaming, or hiding their faces in their arms.

The church should not produce wire-mesh Christians whose primary objective is to be fed and then go elsewhere for comfort and fellowship. If that is the case, then we have created a school rather than a church. The church *body* should be the epitome of interdependent activity.

Ties That Bind—with Many

I once read a description of life that compared it to bouncing on a trampoline which was supported on all four sides by people. The author contended that, like the number of people needed to hold the trampoline, each of us needs the combination of family, relatives, friends, and work associates to lead a stable, well-balanced life. He believed that an emotionally healthy person should have twenty to thirty people supporting the trampoline of life. Paul was aware of this when he reminded us, "For in fact the body is not one member but many" (1 Cor. 12:14).

As Christians, we can learn from this. We need to make a conscious effort to widen our circle of support to include other believers. By weaving the threads of relationship with God's people, we can administer our special gifts to one another.

Heaven/Homeward Bound

Until we are in heaven, we are not truly home. This old earth is temporary and transitory:

For our citizenship is in heaven, from which we also eagerly wait for the Savior, the Lord Jesus Christ. (Phil. 3:20)

No matter where we live now, it's temporary housing. Christians, we are en route to another world—one that's permanent, one that's awesome! We must keep one eye watching where we walk in this world and one eye fixed on heaven.

Some people will say, "Careful! You can be so heavenly-minded that you're no earthly good." I contend that the best way to be of earthly good is to be heavenly-minded.

As believers living in the world, we are bound to experience some loneliness. After all, we're not home yet! Isn't it a mystery how our hearts can yearn for a home we have not yet seen? This should confirm that we are in the world, but we are not of the world. Until we get to our real home, we should remember that what's up ahead is far better that what we've got here. Like Dorothy in the *Wizard of Oz*, we can confidently say, "There's no place like home!"

With this at the center of your awareness, don't settle for a counterfeit or substitute for peace and fulfillment. The fundamental answer to loneliness is a solid, intimate relationship with Jesus Christ. With that in place, make connections with other Christians with whom you can grow. Weave those threads with God and His people. Remember, loneliness is a high price to pay for independence.

Chapter Two

It is impossible to believe that the same God who permitted His own Son to die a bachelor regards celibacy as an actual sin.

—*H. L. Mencken*

Weaving
SuccessFULLY SINGLE Threads

We're all born single. Some choose to remain without a life-mate, although they still weave relational threads with family, friends, and associates. Admittedly, this is not the way of most, but some single people are very content. Mr. Justice McCardie of the British High Court (who is a bachelor himself) said, "A bachelor is a man who looks before he leaps and, having looked, does not leap." Many other single people are *not* so content with their situation. In fact, they're impatiently chomping at the bit, wishing God would just part the clouds and point out the right person to marry.

In the United States, the singleness trend has manifested itself in more single adults than ever before. One third of American households are occupied by one or more single persons. In the San Francisco Bay area, half the population over the age of seventeen is single. The 10,000-member Houston church, Brentwood Baptist, has a burgeoning singles ministry because more than half the adult members are unmarried or divorced. This, unfortunately, is the current trend in post-Ozzie-and-Harriet America.

My intent is not to solve the problem of singleness (clearly, some don't consider it a problem) but to look at living fully as a single person while maximizing your God-given gifts. Whether you will be single forever, or whether the Lord eventually brings you a perfect mate, the goal is to live fully in His light.

Anxiously Waiting?

Have you ever looked in the mirror and reacted with startling thoughts like, "Man, I've got to do something quick! I'm getting more bald on top, and the laugh lines on my face are becoming full-fledged wrinkles. If I don't do something quick, no one will want me. I may never get married!"

Anxiety is further heightened when we compare ourselves to the faces and figures we see on TV, movies, billboards, and magazines. We hear that "thin is in" and conclude that if "stout is out," we may never wed. Even the U.S. Census Bureau contributes to the gloom. According to their statistics, a man who is unmarried at age thirty-five has only a slim chance of ever marrying!

But Jesus told us not to let these concerns lead to worry:

"Therefore do not worry, saying, 'What shall we eat?' or 'What shall we drink?' or 'What shall we wear?'...."Matt. 6:31)

I know it's easier said than done, but He specifically tells us not to be so body-conscious and temporary-minded. Our heavenly Father knows our needs, and worry serves no positive purpose. Thankfully, God's plan for us is not dictated by worldly standards and statistics.

The Slights of Being Single

Single people often feel they are subtly, or not so subtly, put down. Unfortunately, sometimes married Christians deal them a back-of-the-hand blow with comments like, "You know, brother, you can't be truly fulfilled until you're married.

That's God's plan."

In a *New York Times* article written by a radical conservative, no attempt was made to disguise his single prejudice:

> The single man is disposed to criminality, drugs, and violence. He is irresponsible about his debts, he's alcoholic, he's accident prone, venereal diseased. Unless he can marry, he is destined to an unsteady life: solitary, poor, nasty, brutish, and short.

Talk about negativity! This extreme and shocking statement oozes it. But if you are single, you have probably heard your share of narrow-minded, thoughtless comments.

Pressure on single people is nothing new. The ancient Jews believed it was a sin for a man not to have a wife. According to their view, it was one of seven major sins that could actually prevent him from entering heaven. Of course, that was not biblical, but it evolved out of their warped philosophy and culture. While our society would not be so overtly prejudiced, singles are often slighted or disregarded. I like what one eighty-seven-year-old spinster wrote in her will, "I don't want anybody to put 'Miss' on my tombstone—I haven't missed as much as some people think!" Bravo for her!

The Gift of Singleness?

In the Bible, singleness is regarded as a gift. That's right. Even William Shakespeare called celibacy "single blessedness." However, just because you are currently unmarried does not mean you have this "gift." The gift of singleness refers to a voluntarily celibate life, given for the primary purpose of serving God and the kingdom without the distractions of other relationships. In Matthew 19, Jesus spoke about marriage and divorce, which led to an interesting discussion with His disciples about the option of living a single life:

He said to them, "Moses, because of the hardness of your hearts, permitted you to divorce your wives, but from the beginning it was not so. And I say to you, whoever divorces his wife, except for sexual immorality, and marries another, commits adultery; and whoever marries her who is divorced commits adultery." His disciples said to Him, "If such is the case of the man with his wife, it is better not to marry." (Matt. 19:8-10)

His disciples were jolted by that one. They openly wondered if the responsibilities and repercussions of marriage and divorce were so weighty that perhaps it was better not to marry at all. Frankly, marriage is such a serious commitment, I wish more love-struck couples would weigh it carefully before walking to the altar to say their vows. Notice that Jesus didn't tell them that being single was wrong. Instead, He used the conversation as a springboard to endorse God-called singleness:

But He said to them, "All cannot accept this saying, but only those to whom it has been given: For there are eunuchs who were born thus from their mother's womb, and there are eunuchs who were made eunuchs by men, and there are eunuchs who have made themselves eunuchs for the kingdom of heaven's sake. He who is able to accept it, let him accept it." (Matt. 19:11-12)

Jesus said, "...to whom it has been given." There are those to whom God gives the ability to stay on course while handling the unique pressures of the single lifestyle. Jesus knew being single is not for everyone, but He mentioned three groups who could successfully live unmarried, celibate lives:

• Those who, because of a congenital defect, would not be

able to reproduce. These men were called *eunuchs*
("eunuchs who were born thus from their mother's
womb").

- Those who had been physically castrated ("eunuchs who
were made eunuchs by men"). While this is uncommon
today, in ancient times, and especially in pagan cultures,
a man would sometimes rule over a harem of the high
king and the courts. This kind of eunuch was castrated in
order to be trusted in his responsibilities.

- Those who have renounced marriage for the purpose of
serving God more fully ("eunuchs who have made themselves eunuchs for the kingdom of heaven's sake").
Remember, Jesus acknowledged this gift of celibacy isn't
for everyone. That's why He added, "He who is able to
accept it, let him accept it."

Your reaction at this point may be, "Lord, please don't
give me that gift! Call me to be a missionary in the deepest,
darkest jungles of Africa if You want, but I beg You not to
keep me single!" If these are your feelings, you can be sure
that celibacy is not your calling. You'd probably know it by
now if it was. For those who are called to it, singleness will
be comfortable.

One night a little girl overheard her maiden aunt saying
her prayers. The little girl's mother caught her listening and
reprimanded her, saying it was wrong to eavesdrop.

"But Mommy," the girl replied, "Aunt Emma ended
her prayer so funny."

"What did she say?" asked her mother.

"Well, when she finished praying she said, 'World
without men, ah me.'"

Remember, for those who have it, celibacy is not a curse,
but a lifestyle to be respected. Unlike Aunt Emma, when you
possess the gift of celibacy, you are sure of it. There won't be
confused feelings such as, "I really want to be married, but

maybe the Lord wants me to be single, so I'll suffer for God and not marry." Thankfully, God doesn't work that way.

John Stott, one of the great Bible scholars and pastors of our time, has the gift of being single. In the eyes of the Christian world, he is a giant in his ability to teach and convey truth. Now, in his older years, he still has never married. He has forfeited marriage to focus his attention on the things of God's kingdom. His commitment to his individual calling has resulted in a dynamic spiritual life. Single friend, God's plan includes you. Yes, it does!

Good Gifts: Marriage AND Singleness

Almost two thousand years ago, the young Christians of Corinth wanted to understand God's intentions both for marriage and singleness. Paul spoke directly to their concerns:

Now concerning the things of which you wrote to me:
It is good for a man not to touch a woman. (1 Cor. 7:1)

Paul wanted them to know that being single is good, but fornication is not. Jesus confirmed that singleness is a gift, but not everyone should remain single. There is another factor to consider—the temptation factor.

Nevertheless, because of sexual immorality, let each
man have his own wife, and let each woman have her
own husband. (1 Cor. 7:2)

Paul wasn't saying that sexual release should be the reason for marriage. He simply stated that marriage is the norm and our inborn physical desires and needs are met within this relationship. That was God's plan from the beginning: "Two shall become one flesh." Paul respected and understood this. He knew that most people had the desire for a mate. Yet in his own experience, Paul found his life as a single, celibate man so fulfilling, he wished everyone could know his joy:

For I wish that all men were even as I myself. But each one has his own gift from God, one in this manner and another in that. (1 Cor. 7:7)

Because of this, some have speculated that Paul was once married and that his wife left him after his conversion. There is no evidence to support this theory. All we know is he joyfully embraced his celibacy while respecting those with different callings. Paul went on to address the unmarried and the widows, saying:

...It is good for them if they remain even as I am; but if they cannot exercise self-control, let them marry. For it is better to marry than to burn with passion. (1 Cor. 7:8b-9)

This is not a slam on marriage. Taken in context, Paul was responding to a misguided group of people in the Corinthian church who said it was more spiritual to remain single and worship God wholeheartedly than to marry. He corrected them by saying that while he valued *his* life of celibacy, not everyone had the same calling. For those who are not called to celibacy but try to live the life, they will burn with passion, living miserably in a temptation-filled world.

The world of Corinth was especially enticing. Legalized prostitution meant temptation on every corner. A young man simply going about his business had to be prepared to deal with this. Passion, like fire, is a good servant but a bad master. In reminding the people of Corinth of passions and temptations, Paul dealt straight-forwardly with the pluses and minuses of the single life. He wanted them to make wise, informed decisions.

A Deeper Problem: Living Married, Acting Single

The Corinthian movement to stay single regardless of whether they had the calling of celibacy, in order to be more spiritual, incited some married people to divorce. There were also some married people who were trying to live like single people by abstaining from sex with their partners. Paul cautioned married folks of the danger of this practice:

Do not deprive one another except with consent for a time, that you may give yourselves to fasting and prayer; and come together again so that Satan does not tempt you because of your lack of self-control. (1 Cor. 7:5)

Are you married? If so, you must maintain intimacy with your spouse by clearing any stones from the road of communication. Sexual fulfillment within marriage grows out of the relationship of trust and love. I know of couples whose marriage is merely an arrangement of convenience. They're living together under the same roof but not loving each other. Watch out! Don't act like a single, celibate person while living in the same house with your mate. It won't work, and you will be headed for trouble if you think it will.

Paul further cautioned the married, "Are you bound to a wife? Do not seek to be loosed" (1 Cor. 7:27). In other words, be true to the gift of marriage by honoring and upholding it. These are crucial words for today that should be memorized by every couple. There was a time when marriage was regarded as a sacred contract. Today, many think of it as a ninety-day option!

Living Single, Acting Married

Being married and acting single is less common these days than the situation of single people living together as though they were married. This has become the accepted norm. Move in, try it out, get intimate, and see if it all works out. If it doesn't, then just move out and try again. In doing so, people prematurely enjoy the fringe benefits of sexual relations and a shared life without the commitment of marriage.

Modern man speaks of intercourse as "having sex" or "making love" (a misnomer if there ever was one). The Bible never speaks this way. The Scriptures talk of a man "knowing" his wife. Why? Because sex is not a mere act; it is a relationship.

For those called to celibacy, attempting to marry would deprive them of the fruits of a life dedicated to God and His kingdom. In such an arrangement, both lifestyles of marriage and singleness would be compromised.

Paul gave us the solid, humane advice to live true to our gift. He exhorted us to carefully determine whether our gift is marriage or celibacy, and then to live appropriately to honor and fulfill our calling:

> *But I want you to be without care. He who is unmarried cares for the things of the Lord—how he may please the Lord. But he who is married cares about the things of the world—how he may please his wife. (1 Cor. 7:32-33)*

You belong to God. Be true to your God and to your gift. Don't enter into a relationship that would be a source of constant conflict.

Successful Singles from Scripture

People need role models. The Chinese used to say, "Not the cry but the flight of the wild duck leads the flock to fly and follow." Where do we find people who are flying in the right direction? A few years ago, *U.S. News and World Report* stated that celebrities Clint Eastwood and Eddie Murphy were high on the list of role models for single,

American males. Hard to believe, isn't it? In the same way that many little pebbles can determine the course of a stream, many of our decisions are influenced by our role models. We emulate our role model's lifestyle, clothing, speech, and values—until a better (or more popular) role model comes along.

Fortunately, the Bible has given us timeless role models for single living. We don't have to depend on the world's role models or fickle definitions for examples of dynamic, full, successful lives. Although there are many, let's take a look at two successful singles from Scripture: Joseph and Daniel.

Joseph: Coping with Temptation and Isolation

It seems that some people get all the breaks. You know the type—always on top, always favored, and always pampered. Often, these privileged folks don't even earn their status; they're either born into it, or they are just in the right place at the right time.

Joseph was like that. He was an outstanding young man, blessed with extraordinary looks, who was lavishly loved and favored by his dad. His easy good fortune inspired jealousy and fear in his brothers. That's usually the case. People of fragile character just can't stand watching someone else be blessed. Joseph's brothers worried that his dreams of greatness might come true, and one day he would rule over them. To ensure that Joseph's dreams never became reality, they took matters into their own hands by selling him into slavery. To convince their father that his son had been eaten by a wild animal, they brought him Joseph's coat of many colors, which they had dipped in goat's blood. At that point, Joseph's life entered the pressure zone—that place where God uses trial, and even temptation, to temper the core of our being. While still a young, single man, Joseph went from pampered son to persecuted slave.

Coping with Sexual Temptation

In Genesis 39, Joseph's life had drastically changed. He no longer lived the privileged life of a favored son but was a slave of Potiphar, who was an officer of Pharaoh and captain of the guard. Joseph's situation could have been desperately bleak, but the Lord was with him:

The Lord was with Joseph, and he was a successful man; and he was in the house of his master the Egyptian. And his master saw that the Lord was with him and that the Lord made all he did to prosper in his hand. So Joseph found favor in his sight, and served him. Then he made him overseer of his house, and all that he had he put under his authority. So it was, from the time that he had made him overseer of his house and all that he had, that the Lord blessed the Egyptian's house for Joseph's sake; and the blessing of the Lord was on all that he had in the house and in the field. Thus he left all that he had in Joseph's hand, and he did not know what he had except for the bread which he ate. Now Joseph was handsome in form and appearance. (Gen. 39:2-6)

Joseph was described as a godly, seek-first-the-kingdom, single man. He was well-built, handsome, and prospering under circumstances that would have meant depression and destitution to most people. These successful qualities had a magnetic appeal that drew the inappropriate attention of Potiphar's wife. There was no coy hinting around—she wanted Joseph:

And it came to pass after these things that his master's wife cast longing eyes on Joseph, and she said, "Lie with me." (Gen. 39:7)

Now that's what I call overt! No mistaking what she wanted from Joseph. Once I was visiting Bangkok on a teaching trip with the leader of a mission organization. Our first night there, we took a stroll down the streets of the city to walk off the jet lag. Prostitutes emerged from the shadows of buildings and alleys. They followed us, shouting offers of sexual favors for a fee. It was as if clones of Potiphar's wife were roaming the streets! The only reasonable course of action (which we took!) was to do an about-face and quickly get out of sight.

Joseph could have felt flattered by this attention and tempted by the easy opportunity. After all, he was far from home and no one of any consequence could see him. But Joseph knew better. God sees everything, and Joseph lived his life by that principle:

> *But he refused and said to his master's wife, "Look, my master does not know what is with me in the house, and he has committed all that he has to my hand. There is no one greater in this house than I, nor has he kept back anything from me but you, because you are his wife. How then can I do this great wickedness, and sin against God?" (Gen. 39:8-9)*

Foremost in Joseph's mind were his responsibilities to Potiphar, who had entrusted his household to him and his responsibilities to God. To sleep with this woman would have been a fourfold sin:

1. It would be a sin against his own body,
2. It would be a sin against his master's wife,
3. It would be a sin against his master, Potiphar, and most significantly,
4. It would be a sin against God.

Joseph lived for God and, therefore, he was able to handle sexual temptation in a godly way. His methods of coping with this tempting sin were not haphazard.

I heard a story of a man who would occasionally sneak into his neighbor's orchard to pick some fruit from his trees. He would carefully look around to make sure no one was watching. One day his young son was with him. As usual, the man looked to the right and to the left and then prowled his way through the fence. As he was about to help himself to the fruit, his son startled him by crying, "Dad! Dad! You didn't look up! You forgot to see if God is watching." When we are tempted and ready to yield, we need to stop and remember our Master is always watching!

He Who Hesitates—Sins

Why is it that opportunity knocks only once, while temptation constantly bangs on the door? Joseph's trials were not simply one-shot events requiring a single act of faith and self-control. Just as we cope with ongoing temptation, Joseph dealt repeatedly with Potiphar's wife, who would not take "no" for an answer.

> So it was, as she spoke to Joseph day by day, that he did not heed her, to lie with her or to be with her. (Gen. 39:10)

Her strategy was consistent and so was Joseph's resistance. He did not heed or listen to her but kept refusing *without hesitation*. He knew this was the key to resisting temptation. Joseph didn't sit down to consider the situation or try to find a way to make it more palatable, like, "Well, maybe I should just hang around and witness to her or something." Rather than considering the temptation, he consistently, and without hesitation, said no.

33

Martin Luther said, "We cannot prevent the birds from flying over our heads, but we can prevent them from building nests in our hair." That's also true when it comes to temptation. We can't stop the devil from his onslaught, but we can actively resist him. And when you do, "he will flee from you" (James 4:7).

Look Temptation in the Eye—and Run!

Day after day, Joseph was presented with temptation and the opportunity to fall prey to this seductress. In fact, as she made it easier for him to give in, it grew progressively more difficult to resist:

> But it happened about this time, when Joseph went into the house to do his work, and none of the men of the house was inside.... (Gen. 39:11)

No one was there to catch him or see if he did the right thing. Potiphar's wife aggressively took advantage of this opportunity. Eventually, she pulled out all the stops and was totally blunt and aggressive with this young, single man:

> ...that she caught him by his garment, saying, "Lie with me." But he left his garment in her hand, and fled and ran outside. (Gen. 39:12)

Did you catch that? She put the make on him, and his response was to run (or should I say streak?) out of the house. Joseph was so committed to resisting her, that he left his shirt in her hand and ran. Although he lost his shirt, he kept his purity! The Bible tells us to flee temptation, and that's exactly what Joseph did. There may be many good, protective measures for dealing with temptation, but running away from it is a sure winner.

It's no accident that the primary temptation Joseph faced was sexual. Most people, and especially single people, know it's one of the strongest lures in life. Therefore, it is also one of Satan's favorite forms of bait. It could be that this was Joseph's weak spot. Perhaps sexual temptation was hard for him to handle. He knew that the best way to fight it was to flee from it.

Men, remember that. Evaluate your own response to temptation. Do you stop and take a look when you "channel-surf" onto an alluring scene on TV? Do you slow down and glance at those magazines in the convenience store? If that is your weak area, fight it like Joseph did—by fleeing from it. "Ah, that's cowardly," you say. Call it what you will, but it works!

According to Greek myth, as a child, Achilles, the great hero of the Trojan War, was dipped in the waters of the river Styx by his mother, Thetis, in order to make him invincible. As a result, every inch of Achilles' body was invulnerable to wounds, except the heel by which his mother had held him while she dipped him in the river. For many years, Achilles escaped battles unscathed but, eventually, the poisoned arrow of the Trojan, Paris, found his heel and inflicted a death wound.

Satan works that way. He tempts Christians where they are the weakest. Having found their pet inclinations, passions, and desires, he attacks them at their weak spots and is often successful in bringing them down.

You know the weak areas in your life. Everyone feels tempted at times, and that is not a sin. It's when we yield to the temptation by thinking about it, toying and playing with it, that we get in trouble.

Sexuality: Great in Its Place

We need to maintain a balanced viewpoint on the subject of sex so that we are able to see the issue in perspective. Sexual desire and allurement are not evil in themselves. C.S. Lewis reminded us that, "pleasure is God's invention, not the devil's." Sexuality was created by God. It is wonderful and fulfilling in marriage but cheapened and dirty when it takes place under other circumstances. Picture, for example, beautiful roses, trees, and vines growing in the lush, brown dirt of a garden. If we took that rich, beautiful soil and dumped it on the living room carpet, what was lovely and fertile in the setting of the garden becomes inappropriate and filthy in the house. Out of place, it defiles what's around it. Similarly, in the proper context, sex is beautiful, but in the wrong situation, it is cheapened. Single friend, please hold sex as something sacred.

As we grow in Christ, we develop a greater respect for our bodies, which contributes to our desire to keep them from them sin. Sexual passion is like a fire. Inside the fireplace of marriage, we can let it burn hot and passionately, but outside the fireplace it can damage and destroy. Paul, the apostle, spoke to the promiscuous Corinthians about the holiness of our bodies:

> *Or do you not know that your body is the temple of the Holy Spirit, who is in you, whom you have from God, and you are not your own? For you were bought at a price; therefore glorify God in your body and in your spirit, which are God's. (I Cor. 6:19-20)*

Whatever we accept or reject in the way of temptation will affect and, sometimes, control us for the rest of our lives. A small compromise makes a larger compromise easier the next time temptation comes along. Conversely, consistently coping with temptation from a godly perspective without hesitation makes us stronger and less vulnerable.

Joseph: Coping with Isolation

Joseph's troubles were not over immediately simply because he dealt with temptation in a godly way. On the contrary, Potiphar's wife was angry and offended by his rejection.

She retaliated by accusing him of trying to rape her. Victor Hugo was onto something when he said, "Hell hath no fury like a woman scorned." For Joseph, the result was pretty grim. Even after staying faithful to God and maintaining his integrity, Joseph found his situation going from bad to worse:

> *Then Joseph's master took him and put him into the prison, a place where the king's prisoners were confined. And he was there in the prison. (Gen. 39:20)*

Joseph went from being a slave to being a prisoner. In both instances he was without fault, although he suffered consequences as if he were guilty. To outward appearances, his life was going down the tube. Remember, fellow Christian, doing the right thing doesn't always mean instant positive results. The martyrs who gave their lives for what was right would be quick to confirm this.

Joseph was successful in fending off temptation, but consider another enemy of Joseph and the single person: Isolation.

Trust: the Secret Weapon

When Joseph was put in prison, he must have been at an all-time low in his life. His confinement presented him with a huge challenge to trust and remain faithful in spite of his circumstances. He could have complained that life wasn't fair; he could have become bitter and refused fellowship with God; or he could have trusted an unknown future to a known God—which is exactly what he did:

> *But the Lord was with Joseph and showed him mercy, and He gave him favor in the sight of the keeper of the prison. And the keeper of the prison committed to Joseph's hand all the prisoners who were in the prison; whatever they did there, it was his doing. The keeper of the prison did not look into anything that*

*was under Joseph's authority, because the Lord was
with him; and whatever he did, the Lord made it
prosper. (Gen. 39:21-23)*

Joseph knew that trust was the secret weapon in dealing
with adversity and isolation. His reliance on the Lord brought
God near and encouraged Joseph to believe that God would
bless him even under negative circumstances. He didn't wal-
low in self-pity. He didn't become bitter and hardened or sit by
passively. He acted on his trust by making the best of his situation. He may have silently reasoned, "If I have to be a prisoner, I'm going to be the best prisoner this place has ever seen!
I'll excel as a slave and let God use this situation for His glory."

This is an attitude that's hard for most of us to fathom—
similar to the story of the optimistic little boy who woke up
one morning only to find a backyard full of manure. To his
family's surprise, his eyes lit up and he jumped up and down
in delight. His brother asked him, "Are you crazy? What are
you so happy about?" The little boy didn't hesitate. "With all
this manure, there's got to be a pony around here somewhere!" Gratefully, our trust is better founded than this.

Joseph's successful attitude was noticed immediately by the
guard who began entrusting responsibilities to him that
improved his life. Notice that God didn't immediately zap
Joseph out of prison, but He brought blessings and opportunities
to him in his current situation.

Isolation is one of the most difficult barriers single people face. In the quiet of loneliness, problems loom larger than
life, and even God can seem to recede into the distance.
Whether, like Joseph, we are dealing with the attack of being
treated badly or wrongly accused, or coping with ongoing
singleness when our heart yearns for marriage, the secret
weapon is drawing near to God in trust.

Daniel: Single to the Max

Let's fast-forward to the Babylonian captivity of Judah—another period in time when single living wasn't easy. During this period, hundreds of the finest single people were ushered off to this foreign country for the purpose of serving as the elite guardians under the tyrant, Nebuchadnezzar. Kidnapped, and 650 miles away from his home, Daniel was little more than a face on a milk carton. In this pagan setting, living as a single person with integrity and moral values was no easy task. He was, in many ways, like a college student on his own for the first time. Daniel was an intellectually sharp young man who used his single life as a unique opportunity to glorify God.

Prospering without Compromise

Because of Daniel's natural attributes, he was given an opportunity to serve in the special officers' corps. Along with three other young men, Daniel was brought to the palace to study for three years prior to serving in the king's court. These young men were the cream of the crop physically and intellectually. As a reward and a show of faith in their capabilities, the king provided them with meals of the very same delicacies and wine he himself ate and drank:

> *And the king appointed for them a daily provision of the king's delicacies and of the wine which he drank, and three years of training for them, so that at the end of that time they might serve before the king....But Daniel purposed in his heart that he would not defile himself with the portion of the king's delicacies, nor with the wine which he drank; therefore he requested of the chief of the eunuchs that he might not defile himself. (Dan. 1:5, 8)*

Daniel wasn't trying to be hardheaded. Even in this coveted position, uppermost in his mind was that he was a Jew, a part of God's covenant people. His primary concern was remaining true and obedient to his God by eating only kosher foods so he wouldn't be ceremonially defiled. Daniel made a request to the chief of the eunuchs that he and his three companions be allowed to eat their diet of vegetables and water. This could have been construed as an insult to the king. And if Daniel and his friends failed to thrive on their different diet, it could have meant punishment for the master of the eunuchs. Daniel was going against the norm, fighting city hall, and standing up to that looming giant of "peer pressure."

Pressure from peers to conform and compromise standards are still the greatest problems facing young people today. Ronald Hutchcraft, of Youth for Christ International, believes there are seven unique pressures facing today's young people:

1. Unparalleled media bombardment: The media transmits more than entertainment; it imparts values.

2. Pressure to make moral choices at a young age: Kids are confronted with drugs and sex earlier than ever. It is estimated that one in five junior high school students has already had premarital sex.

3. Pessimism for the future: Teenagers today fear that "something's gonna get us"—either disease, global warming, or someone pushing a button that sends the world up in smoke.

4. Absence of moral consensus: There are fewer taboos today and, therefore, there is an absence of a sense of violation.

5. Changes in the structure of the home: A rising number of fragmented families adds to the moral confusion among the young, who may be lacking strong family support.

6. Unprecedented freedom: Teens, and even younger children, are away from home and without supervision more than ever before.

7. Emotional softness: Because life has been easier for this generation, there is an inability to cope with pain. Instant gratification and the absence of discomfort have created an emotional weakness that makes them unfit for the real world.

These trends are frightening but not insurmountable. It's still possible to stem the tide of this pressure and to love and obey God in the midst of a society that doesn't. Remember, Daniel was a teenager away from the moral support of his family and his worship center. Smack dab in the middle of pressured paganism, he stood strong for his God.

Independent, but Not Alone

It wasn't long before Nebuchadnezzar began having disturbing dreams. He demanded that his magicians, astrologers, sorcerers, and the Chaldeans not only interpret the dream but, incredibly, tell him the dream itself. Without exception, they insisted that the king's request was impossible. In anger, Nebuchadnezzar decreed that all wise men would be killed. Young Daniel was considered a part of this elite group, but he hadn't yet been consulted. When Daniel learned that he and his friends were also in danger, he approached the king, asking for some time. He would then tell the king both his dream and its interpretation.

After Daniel was given permission, he quickly rallied his companions and friends for a prayer meeting. Although he made his difficult decision privately with the Lord, he then sought the support of his friends:

Then Daniel went to his house, and made the decision known to Hananiah, Mishael, and Azariah, his companions, that they might seek mercies from the God of heaven concerning this secret, so that Daniel and his companions might not perish with the rest of the wise men of Babylon. (Dan. 2:17-18)

As tenacious and godly as Daniel was, he did not go it alone. Facing a dangerous situation, he relied on God, but he also consulted his network of friends. Daniel volunteered for this hazardous duty of interpreting the dream. He had prayed about it, but he also wanted the support and prayers of his friends. And then he was there on center stage—prime time in the palace. God used him in a mighty way as he told the king his dream and its correct interpretation.

The lesson is crystal clear. We are meant to be interdependent. Everyone needs love, acceptance, and encouragement. Friends and other believers serve as a vital link strengthening the life-chain for single adults. Friendships keep us emotionally fit and flexible. They even serve as a safety net, helping us avoid mistakes such as premature marriages or inappropriate relationships. God never intended for us to be Lone Rangers, isolated from fellowship and support. And, thinking back on that old television show, it was Tonto, his faithful friend, who helped old "Lone" out of many a tight spot.

Solomon was right when he said:

As iron sharpens iron, so a man sharpens the countenance of his friend. (Prov. 27:17)

Defiantly Obedient to God

Success can be a magnet that draws people close, but it can also evoke jealousy and envy. When someone is promoted in the company, others seethe with envy because they weren't chosen.

Daniel experienced this kind of envy. His commitment to God brought about a measure of success that created some real problems among his colleagues. In fact, their jealousy was so poisonous, the governors conspired to destroy Daniel by passing a law they knew he would break. The governors proposed and passed a decree banning public prayer to anyone other than King Darius. The penalty of breaking the law was death. In keeping the law, Daniel would have to compromise his beliefs and relationship with God.

> "All the governors of the kingdom, the administrators and satraps, the counselors and advisors, have consulted together to establish a royal statute and to make a firm decree, that whoever petitions any god or man for thirty days, except you, O king, shall be cast into the den of lions." (Dan. 6:7)

> Now when Daniel knew that the writing was signed, he went home. And in his upper room, with his windows open toward Jerusalem, he knelt down on his knees three times a day, and prayed and gave thanks before his God, as was his custom since early days. (Dan. 6:10)

Did you catch that? To pray publicly in Babylon during that month brought capital punishment. But Daniel was defiant in his intention to remain openly obedient to God. Was he being ostentatious or reactive? Was he trying to rub their noses in his personal righteousness? Not at all. He was simply doing what he had always done. He didn't suddenly begin praying; it had been "his custom since early days." Daniel had been faithful to God since he was a young boy, so why stop now? This is the value of consistent devotion: it leads to the ability to stand tall when the pressure to bow is on!

Daniel certainly had other options. He could have rational-ized, "Perhaps I'll just lay low for thirty days. I can still pray if I do it in a secret place. After all, 'religion is a private thing.'" He could have closed his windows and, in private, opened his heart. But not Daniel. He knew his life was at stake and, sure enough, it wasn't long before he was in the lions' den. Even the prospect of death was not more important than living in obedi-ence to God. Daniel believed it was better to die for a convic-tion than to live with a compromise! God honored Daniel's obe-dience by sending His angel to miraculously shut the lions' mouths.

Single people face the world's lions' den constantly. There are pressures to be "swinging singles" or, at the other extreme, to mope around like members of a lonely hearts club. Don't fall for either of these traps! Paul reminds us:

And do not be conformed to this world, but be trans-formed by the renewing of your mind.... (Rom. 12:2)

Or, as J.B. Phillips puts it in his excellent paraphrased translation:

Don't let the world around you squeeze you into its own mold, but let God remake you so that your whole attitude of mind is changed.

We don't have to compromise and be pushed into either mold. Apart from God, the worldly definition of success will bring only frustration and loneliness. There comes a time when, like Daniel, we have to risk the world's rejection by defiant obedience to God.

Maximum Singleness

As a single person, Daniel used his gifts and talents to the maximum. There is no disqualification from serving God because of our marital status. The New Testament question is not, Are you married or are you single? It is, Do you belong to Jesus Christ?

Corrie ten Boom was a single woman who dynamically affected the world by hiding Jews from the Nazis during World War II. Her walk with the Lord enabled her to live courageously, selflessly, and fully. She faced trials most of us cannot imagine, and she emerged victorious, ready to share her life and her Lord with the world. Could anyone dare suggest that her life was less than complete because she lived as a single person? She was a kingdom-seeker who now, most certainly, lives in the very presence of the King.

We might call Corrie and Daniel "thermostat believers" as opposed to "thermometer believers." A thermometer is regulated by its surroundings and simply reflects the current weather. A thermostat, however, is the regulator of its surroundings. It doesn't go up or down in accordance with weather changes but stays steady and regular. Pressure is everywhere, but the culture shouldn't dictate our standards.

All rivers have one thing in common: they're crooked. Think about the last time you saw a straight-as-an-arrow river. Though no two have identical flow patterns, they are all meandering. Why? The answer is simple: water. As it seeks its own level, it takes the path of least resistance. A river flows around anything that blocks it. Life is the same way. If we simply "go with the flow" of this world, taking the path of least resistance and bending with peer pressure, we'll eventually find we are living a very crooked life! Don't bow to the altar of the media, universities, or politicians. Let God mold you into an effective single person who can go against the flow.

While You Wait—Live!

Jesus told His anxious disciples to occupy until He comes (Luke 19:13). Stretching that principle just a bit further, we could also say to those who are waiting for Prince or Princess

Charming, "Be occupied with living fully, walking in the Spirit, exercising your gifts and talents. The Lord knows your needs and you know what? He will fulfill them in His time!"

Anne Kimel wrote a great little piece about this waiting period entitled, "I Gave God Time."

> I gave God time and room and space. He worked to create in me, His child, a more quiet, centered place. A deeper root of peace and trust. He never fails to come through. Jesus, if this is Your will, then yes to being single. In my deepest heart I want to marry, to belong to a great man, to know that I am linked to his life and he to mine following Christ and our dreams together. But You know what I need, Lord. If I never marry, it is yes to You.

Are you willing to trust God to this extent? Anne is now married, but when she was single, her attitude was one of obedience to God's will. God provided for her and, single friend, God will provide for you.

While you are single, you are in a blessed partnership with the Lord. Remember that your Partner is your daily source of comfort and strength. He is the very same God who unlocked prison doors, elevated slaves to influential rulers, and miraculously clamped shut the jaws of ravenous lions.

Go about your business, living with enthusiasm and confident trust. Only you can make your unique contribution to the kingdom of God. Walk with Him—trust in Him—say "yes" to your life right now.

Chapter Three

By the time teenagers begin dating, much of the preparation their parents can give them has already been done. Their attitudes toward the opposite sex began forming when they were in the cradle.
                                                                    —*Josh McDowell*

The Weaving Begins: Dating

D ating, with all its problems and joys, can be a challenge to the most confident young person. In my pastoring, I have become aware that there is much confusion and misunderstanding surrounding the issues of dating and love. Questions cover a wide range of concerns, such as:

- Is dating biblical?
- What is wrong with premarital sex with someone you love?
- What are the chances of dating success between a believer and a nonbeliever?
- What's the difference between infatuation and love?

We will look at these and other issues from the vantage point of God's intentions for men and women and what the Bible tells us about this important part of our lives.

What the Bible Tells Us about Dating

We will not find "Thou shalt not date" written anywhere in the Bible. Nor will we find "Thus saith the Lord, this is *how* thou shalt date." In studying a subject like this, we look at biblical examples, drawing principles and models from them for our own behavior. Taking cultural differences into account, there is much we can learn by looking at the roots of certain practices.

During biblical times, Jewish parents solved the dating dilemma by prearranging marriages for their children. Sometimes, if the parents determined that the union would be beneficial for both families, the betrothal took place when the future bride and groom were babies. Certainly, they took into consideration the attributes they wanted in their future daughter-in-law or son-in-law. Parents of the bride probably hoped for a strong provider, while the groom's parents may have envisioned a lovely young woman who would be a good mother.

When the boy's father found a suitable young woman, he would then choose a go-between, called "the friend of the bridegroom," to assist in the negotiations. A dowry was determined. When negotiations were completed and an agreement reached, the parents of the couple sealed their arrangement, surprisingly, over a cup of coffee.

Then, when the couple was of the appropriate age, the one year engagement period began. With the onset of the engagement, the couple started the dating and courting process—a little backwards to our way of thinking! Although they were not yet married, this betrothal was binding and indicated that neither was available to other suitors. If either person chose to separate during this period, they had to go through the process of a legal divorce.

While this may seem like an ancient approach to marriage, there are some countries, such as India, China, Thailand, and the Philippines, that even today maintain the custom of parents choosing mates for their children. This practice is confidently defended because they have found that when children know they are going to spend their lives with someone, their commitment to the relationship begins at an early age. There must be something to this practice because divorce is almost nonexistent in these countries.

The Bible's Dating Hall of Fame—and Shame

As mentioned earlier, the Bible doesn't specifically discuss dating. However, through biblical characters, we are able to learn much about the process of finding and keeping the mate God has for us.

Isaac: A Lesson in the Power of Praying for a Mate

In the Old Testament book of Genesis, we read that Abraham decided his son, Isaac, should have a wife. He summoned the oldest servant and told him to go to his country and, with God's guidance, find a wife for Isaac. Abraham did not want Isaac's wife chosen from the Canaanites but from among his kindred in his own country. The servant agreed in spite of his worries that a woman who didn't know him or his master might be reluctant to follow him back. Abraham told his servant that God would "send His angel before you, and you shall take a wife for my son from there" (Gen. 24:7).

The servant set out on his journey. He came to a nice little city and stopped to get water for himself and his camels. He must have wondered just how he was supposed to find the perfect wife for Isaac among all of the strangers. In Genesis 24 we see that he prayed an unusual prayer:

> *Then he said, "O Lord God of my master Abraham, please give me success this day, and show kindness to my master Abraham. Behold, here I stand by the well of water, and the daughters of the men of the city are coming out to draw water. Now let it be that the young woman to whom I say, 'Please let down your pitcher that I may drink,' and she says, 'Drink, and I will also give your camels a drink'—let her be the one You have*

appointed for Your servant Isaac. And by this I will know that You have shown kindness to my master." And it happened, before he had finished speaking, that behold, Rebekah, who was born to Bethuel, son of Milcah, the wife of Nahor, Abraham's brother, came out with her pitcher on her shoulder. (Gen. 24:12-15)

The words were not out of his mouth when beautiful Rebekah came out to draw water. The servant's heart was probably beating out of his chest when he asked her for a drink of water. She immediately complied:

So she said, "Drink, my lord." Then she quickly let her pitcher down to her hand, and give him a drink. And when she had finished giving him a drink, she said, "I will draw water for your camels also, until they have finished drinking." (Gen. 24:18-19)

Now, that's an answer to prayer! Don't you know he mentally shouted, "Bingo!" But the servant hesitated a moment, as if to test these circumstances one more moment in the light of God's will.

And the man, wondering at her, remained silent so as to know whether the Lord had made his journey prosperous or not. (Gen. 24:21)

He managed to be invited back to Rebekah's home, where he described his mission to the household. Rebekah's father, Bethuel, was a greedy man who looked outside and saw the dowry of camels and other riches and warmed quickly to the idea. Rebekah, however, was not just shuffled away without being consulted. They asked her if she wanted to go, and she replied simply, "I will go."

Then Rebekah and her maids arose, and they rode on the camels and followed the man. So the servant took Rebekah and departed. Now Isaac came from the way of Beer Lahai Roi, for he dwelt in the South. And Isaac went out to meditate in the field in the evening; and he lifted his eyes and looked, and there, the camels were coming. Then Rebekah lifted her eyes, and when she saw Isaac she dismounted from her camel; for she had said to the servant, "Who is this man walking in the field to meet us?" And the servant said, "It is my master." So she took a veil and covered herself. And the servant told Isaac all the things that he had done. (Gen. 24:61-66)

During this time, Isaac had not been passively waiting for his father's servant to return. He was out in the field *meditating*, a Hebrew word meaning "to seek the Lord in solitude." In other words, he was praying. His courtship was progressing according to the customs of his time, and Isaac was actively involved and interested. However, he was not so frantic in his search that he forgot to seek the Lord. Isaac's prayers were answered: "...and he took Rebekah and she became his wife, and he loved her...." (Gen. 24:67).

Jacob: A Lesson in Waiting Patiently for Your Love

The Lord works differently in each of our lives. God worked quickly, to say the least, in answering Abraham's prayer for a bride for Isaac. Many people would love to have their prayers answered as quickly and with such clarity! Wouldn't it be great to pray, "Lord, send me a wife" and, before you could take a breath, she appeared?

Isaac's son, Jacob, had quite a different experience in marrying his wife. Jacob already knew who he wanted to marry—a beautiful young lady named Rachel. Jacob went to her father, Laban, and asked him what he must do to have his daughter. Laban told Jacob that he must first work for him for seven years. Jacob agreed, but after the seven year period, Laban deceived him by substituting his oldest daughter instead of Rachel under the wedding veil. Jacob was already married when he learned the truth. He wanted Rachel so badly, he agreed to work for Laban another seven years in order to win the right to marry her.

After fourteen years of work, Jacob married Rachel—not exactly a quick courtship. Most people would be depressed to think about waiting fourteen years for the one they wanted to marry. However, the Scripture says that to Jacob, "...they seemed only a few days to him because of the love he had for her" (Gen. 29:20).

Love is willing to wait. 1 Corinthians 13 says love is patient (longsuffering). When couples say, "We want to get married now—we can't wait!" that's exactly the time they need to slow down. Some couples don't want to wait because they're afraid their relationship might not stand the test of time. As we've seen here, God's timing might be quick, or He might want us to wait. Whatever the circumstances, we should be willing to test the relationship and wait for God's timing.

Samson: Lessons through the Eyes of a Dating Failure

Samson was an amazing guy—a virtual superman of the Old Testament. He made Schwarzenegger look like a lightweight. Samson ripped a lion apart with his bare hands; he killed a thousand men with the jawbone of a donkey; and he once tore the metal gates of the city out of the ground and ran up the hill of Hebron with them on his shoulders. Some lift weights, but Samson lifted gates! He was a strong, virile giant of a man whose God-given strength did not compensate for his moral weakness. This frailty showed in his inability to establish a long-term, meaningful relationship with a woman.

He was ruled by lust, pride, and selfishness. In his dating and married life, Samson was a failure. Like many people, he thought these were areas he could handle without God.

Samson Sees: A Daughter of a Philistine

The Philistines were enemies of the Israelites, but that didn't prevent Samson from pursuing a Philistine woman:

Now Samson went down to Timnah, and saw a woman in Timnah of the daughters of the Philistines. (Judg. 14:1)

God had told Samson not to look for a wife among the Philistines or the Canaanites because He would give him one from his own people. But Samson didn't care about God's plan or timing:

So, he went up and told his father and mother, saying, "I have seen a woman in Timnah of the daughters of the Philistines; now therefore, get her for me as a wife." (Judg. 14:2)

Samson was determined to have what he wanted. He didn't consult his parents, he *told* them what he wanted and ordered them to do as he said. They resisted and reminded him that the woman was not one of their own:

Then his father and mother said to him, "Is there no woman among the daughters of your brethren, or among all my people, that you must go and get a wife from the uncircumcised Philistines?" And Samson said to his father, "Get her for me, for she pleases me well." (Judg. 14:3)

Samson got what he wanted, but his new bride caused him nothing but problems. Because she was not loyal to him, she nagged and double-crossed him. As a result of her disloyalty,

Samson angrily killed thirty men. Thinking that Samson thoroughly hated her now, his wife's father gave her to another man. Following a dramatic series of attacks and revenge for the attacks, Samson's marriage ended in disaster when his wife and her father were burned to death.

Samson Sees: A Harlot

You would think after such trauma Samson would turn his heart toward God for guidance with women. But Samson's *eyes* were still in control of his judgment:

Now Samson went to Gaza and saw a harlot there, and went in to her. (Judg. 16:1)

Samson went to Gaza where he saw a pretty woman who was a harlot, and he slept with her. The encounter sounds as though it was no more meaningful than a one-night stand.

Samson Sees: Delilah

Following the brief detour in Gaza, Samson fell in love with Delilah, another Philistine woman. *Delilah* means "lustful," a name she probably acquired because of the jeering comments men made about her. Once again, Samson looked at her and thought he was in love. He was not in love, he was in lust: "Afterward it happened that he loved a woman in the Valley of Sorek, whose name was Delilah" (Judg. 16:4). Samson's problem with lust and his willfulness had led him into his third tragic relationship.

Delilah became obsessed with finding the secret to Samson's great strength. She wanted to report back to the lords of the Philistines who had encouraged her to entice this information from Samson:

And the lords of the Philistines came up to her and said to her, "Entice him, and find out where his great strength lies, and by what means we may overpower him, that we may bind him to afflict him; and every one of us will give you eleven hundred pieces of silver." (Judg. 16:5)

Obviously, Delilah didn't love Samson. She wanted only to trap him and get money from the Philistines. Mighty Samson was too weak to see this.

Samson Sees: Tantalizing Temptations

Delilah did her best to learn the secret to Samson's strength: "Please tell me where your great strength lies, and with what you may be bound to afflict you" (Judg. 16:6). Samson played with this temptation and pretended to comply:

And Samson said to her, "If they bind me with seven fresh bowstrings, not yet dried, then I shall become weak, and be like any other man." (Judg. 16:7)

So, she bound him with bow strings, the Philistines came, and Samson easily broke free and beat them up. Again, she asked the true secret of his strength and, once more, he gave her a false answer which she tested. The Philistines came and, once again, Samson beat them up. Delilah was getting angry. She accused him of lying to her:

Delilah said to Samson, "Until now you have mocked me and told me lies. Tell me what you may be bound with." And he said to her, "If you weave the seven locks of my head into the web of the loom"—(Judg. 16:13-14a)

For the third time, he saw the temptation coming. He knew what she wanted, and he saw what the enemies were doing! But he let her continue. He was flirting with temptation and with his own downfall. Eventually, he succumbed to Delilah's temptations and revealed the secret of his strength.

His pride in his own strength blinded him, his lustful desires blinded him and, eventually, his sin literally blinded him.

Since You've Asked: Dating Questions & Answers

The dating examples from the Bible serve as guideposts for us today. Yet our American culture is vastly different from the cultures of the Old Testament. To help clarify some of today's love and dating concerns, let's take them one by one.

Q. Is dating a good thing to do?

A. A man who counseled singles for many years once said, "I can always tell when it's prom time because I hear from twenty to thirty devastated young girls who didn't get asked. Their self-esteem is at an all-time low because they wanted a date and didn't get one."

This is the flip side of dating. Feelings of rejection and disappointment are real possibilities when we wait for an invitation that doesn't come or we like someone who doesn't return our interest.

Another anti-dating point of view argues that dating is not healthy because it encourages us to put on a mask. We look, act, and smile our very best. Then, after the wedding, there's a difficult period of adjustment when the couple is no longer on its best behavior. The realities of bad breath, bad moods, bills, and our "real" behavior tend to take the stars out of our eyes.

We need to be aware of these pitfalls as we enter the dating game. Every time we extend ourselves to someone, we are exposed to risk. Without becoming cynical, we have to be prepared to take the bumps and bruises as we travel the dating road to find true love. We can also reduce the possibility of heartache and problems by confining our dating to other believers.

Q. How is Christian dating different?

A. For Christians, dating can be a wonderful time of laying an emotional and spiritual foundation. We have the opportunity to determine what kind of person we want to spend our lives with in marriage. Jesus talked about the permanent commitment of marriage:

"So then, they are no longer two but one flesh. Therefore what God has joined together, let not man separate." (Matt. 19:6)

Therefore, dating should not be taken lightly but dealt with soberly and with wisdom.

Whether or not the person you are dating becomes *your* spouse, he or she will most likely be *someone's* spouse one day. Right now, someone could be dating your future spouse. How would you want him or her to be treated? Kindly, of course, and with reverence and respect. Regardless of the situation, dating should be a time of fun and enjoyment, always keeping in mind our responsibilities to one another.

Q. I'm tired of waiting. When is God going to give me my mate?

A. It is important that we don't get so frantic to find a mate that we forget to seek the Lord and His kingdom first, and then let Him add a love relationship to our lives. Just as Isaac's father provided a wife through the guidance of God, your heavenly Father has a wife or husband chosen for you and will bring him or her to you at the right time.

If we become obsessed with looking for a mate, there can be a destructive effect on other important relationships. Every time we meet someone, we wonder, "Is this the one, Lord?" Our vision is clouded with this concern and this can diminish the pure joy of fellowship with others. So, while we should be actively involved in finding our mate, we should guard our thoughts and make sure the Lord is in control.

I struggled with this frustration when I was single. I wanted to be married, and I would pray, "Lord, when are You going to provide?" I was completely focused on my own will and my desire to find a wife. During this time, I came across Psalm 37:4, which says, "Delight yourself also in the Lord, and He shall give you the desires of your heart." This was a turning point that allowed me to let go of the frustration of trying to find a mate and rest in the comfort of seeking the Lord and delighting in Him. Eventually, my heart became pure, and God blessed me with a wife.

It's such a temptation to delight only in ourselves and our desires. But when our desires conform with God's will, our lives become harmonious. If you are overly anxious about finding a mate, try putting matters in perspective by praying, "Lord, I'm going to seek You because You know best and have the best timing for bringing my special someone into my life. I'm going to be actively involved and open to Your leading, but I'm not going to destroy my fellowship with others and become unproductive. Thank You for ordering the steps of my life, Lord."

Q. I really like this girl, but I'm not sure I'm in love with her. Could she be the one for me?

A. When I was a young Christian, and before I met my beautiful wife, I was engaged to another girl. I was infatuated with her, but I wasn't in love with her. Thankfully, we became aware that our feelings were not love, and we both avoided the pitfall of settling for second best.

While infatuation can be the beginning of a true love relationship, in some cases it never progresses. According to one study, the average person "falls in love" five times between ninth grade and the second year of college. This can make sorting out the difference between infatuation and love very tricky. Some of the emotions of infatuation and love are similar. The major difference is that love will stand the test of time, developing a through-thick-and-thin commitment, while infatuation will not.

When I met my wife, I was infatuated and attracted to her, but I knew I *loved* her when, after three years, I was still attracted to her but even more committed. Love stands the test of time.

Q. Is it okay to date an unbeliever?
A. Before we discuss dating between a believer and an unbeliever, let's look at how the Bible regards the situation of a believer joined in marriage to an unbeliever:

Do not be unequally yoked together with unbelievers. For what fellowship has righteousness with lawlessness? And what communion has light with darkness? (2 Cor. 6:14)

The Revised Standard Version says it like this:

Do not be mismated with unbelievers. For what communion is light with darkness or what part has a believer with an unbeliever?

The "unequal yoke" in this verse refers to a marriage between two people who are spiritually different. If a believer in Jesus Christ is married to someone who does not believe, there will be problems.

Some think that the term "unequally yoked" refers to a warning not to marry someone of a different race. God is concerned about our hearts and the spiritual condition of marriages and homes. If a man and woman of different races marry, they should realize they will be confronted with prejudice and other obstacles. But above all else, God wants us to be joined in marriage to someone who loves the Lord as we do.

To understand the consequences of being unequally yoked, it helps to have a better understanding of this analogy. In the time this Scripture was written, farmers harnessed two oxen together with a wooden cross-piece so they could work together pulling a plow. The wise farmer selected two animals of the same species, strength, and temperament, so they could comfortably bear the weight of the yoke while pulling equal amounts of weight at the same pace. To yoke an ox to a pony was not only painful and unproductive, it was cruel. The fundamental differences in their forms and natural inclinations, caused each of them to be limited and impaired by the other.

This is a strong image when applied to an unbeliever yoked in marriage to a believer. Their journey through life can only be a painful struggle and a tug of war. The believer will never be able to fulfill all that God intends for him or her, and there are no guarantees that the unbeliever will be won to Christ through the process. If we are to experience the best and the highest God has for us, we must marry only in the Lord.

The argument might be made, "But we're not getting married, we're just dating!" Guess what? Dating can lead to marriage! So, it follows that it's wrong to date an unbeliever. If you just want a friendship, that's fine, but not a dating relationship that might lead to marriage. In maintaining friendships with unbelievers, we have the opportunity to win them to Christ. But God does not need or want you to date for that reason. Dating is preparation for marriage.

There is a term called "missionary dating" which refers to the misguided strategy of dating an unbeliever with the goal of leading that person to Christ. Sometimes it may work, but it is the exception rather than the rule. Usually, instead of the unbeliever being lifted up, the believer is dragged down.

I do believe, however, that it is wrong to completely sever

friendships with unbelievers and become so isolated we are not feeling the pulse of their lives. As believers, we're called to be salt and light to the world. We can't perform those vital functions if we refuse to be around non-Christians.

Dating, however, is not for the purpose of saving souls. Dating enables us to decide what kind of person we want to spend our lives with and prepares us for that life-long commitment.

Q. What's wrong with premarital sex with someone you love?

A. We've all heard the saying, "too much too soon." Generally, this describes a situation in which someone received privileges before they were fully able to understand and appreciate them. For example, if a young man inherited a great deal of money and property but had never had to work for anything, he would not realize their value or appreciate this gift. In such a situation, what could have been a blessing could actually lead to his downfall.

In dating relationships, becoming "too close too soon" has the same effect. We are not able to appreciate the joys of becoming one flesh in a sexual relationship until a marriage commitment has been made to honor and cement the union. Prior to that, like the young man who received the rewards of labor without working, the gift of sex outside of marriage can actually ruin a relationship.

Although sex without marriage is sometimes called free love or free sex, there's nothing free about it. It costs—big time. Emotionally, it costs by muddying the relationship and confusing our feelings, and spiritually, it drains us of our closeness and fellowship with the Lord. While some people engage in premarital sex in an attempt to cement their love, studies show that it's actually more likely to cause the breakup of the relationship. Jim Burns, pastor and author, wrote of a couple whose promising relationship ended in just this way:

When I first met Linda, I knew that she'd be a real asset to our youth group. She was enthusiastic and fun-loving. When it came to talking seriously about our faith in Christ, she could settle down and really dig into the Scriptures. It was a joy to be around her. Now, two and one half years later, Linda sat in my office and sobbed uncontrollably. Her story went something like this:

Although she dated in high school, she had never been serious about anyone until Tony came along. Tony was in the leadership corps at church. He was popular at school, active in student government, and a real gentleman. At first, most of their dates were double dates or church functions. Very quickly, they both fell head over heels for each other. For Linda, life began to revolve around Tony and the time that they spent together. A few weeks passed into months, and the perfect couple began to spend more and more time together. After youth group, instead of going out with the rest of the kids, they would make an excuse and end up spending an hour or so kissing. They both had high moral standards, but they were so much in love that over the next few months, they found themselves slipping. In Linda's words they went from, "light kissing to heavy kissing, to light petting, to very heavy petting." Slowly but surely, their dates changed from doing fun and active things to situations in which they could be close. Almost every date was filled with very heavy petting.

Sometimes Tony and Linda would talk about their relationship. Although they both were in high school and wanted to go to college, marriage was a possibility. Now, however, both Linda and Tony felt guilty about their physical relationship. They tried to talk about it, but it was a difficult subject to discuss. Although they both tried to stop being so physical, it was getting harder and harder for them to stop. They found themselves communicating less verbally and more sexually.

The Linda who now sat in my office was a serious young woman struggling with guilt and confusion. It was difficult for her to share her experiences. She and Tony had been, in her words, "going all the way" for about two months. The night before, Tony had opened up to her and shared his true inner feelings. He loved her, but he felt a tremendous guilt about their physical relationship. School was going badly, and he wanted to be more involved with church. Although he loved Linda, he felt that the best thing to do was to break up. Linda was crushed, yet she knew that most of what Tony said was true, and now she came to my office looking for answers.

The following letter strips away any romantic notions of premarital sex:

> We had sexual relations before we married; we lived together before we married; I had all four of my children before we married. I sure have reaped a lot for my sin. My children have had to endure the painful storms I brought upon them. I'm so sorry—so very sorry for this. We are all making it because the Lord has carried us—even when we had to go through rough waters. The Lord is so good! I have never had a wedding. I've never known how it is to make love to my husband on our wedding night (instead of before). I have not known what it is like to carry a child and have my husband put his ear to my stomach to feel and hear the baby kick. I have never known what it is like for a

man to ask in a most loving, godly way for my hand in marriage. I have never known a honeymoon. How I long to wear a wedding gown and exchange the words God gives us to say to one another. I will never know these wonderful, beautiful things that the Lord wanted me to have. I did not know. I'm so sorry—my heart hurts so badly. I'm sorry I did not wait for God's best.

Another young woman's anger and hurt come through loud and clear:

I feel mad. I feel cheap. I have high standards, and now I don't even like him. How could I have given so much of my body to someone I thought I liked, but now I can't stand? I sure didn't count the cost.

That's insight, but unfortunately, it came a little too late. If you've already blown it, take heart. Ask God to forgive you and to give you the strength to resist temptation in the future. Don't beat yourself up, but set your sights firmly ahead. Paul says in Philippians 3:13, "...but one thing I do, forgetting those things which are behind and reaching forward to those things which are ahead."

The truth is, it's not easy to maintain a pure relationship without becoming physically involved. The more you love and care for each other, the more difficult it is to resist premature sexual involvement. But God rewards obedience, and you will be rewarded for a lifetime by waiting until marriage to give each other the gift of yourselves.

Q. Does God have a perfect mate picked out for me?

A. This question comes up frequently. My answer is, "No, and yes. No one is perfect, and yes, I believe God has someone specifically picked out for you to bring you to complete fulfillment."

For some, the idea of finding their perfect mate has become confused with finding a "perfect" person. The checklist of the desired qualities can be so long, the person would have to be able to leap tall buildings in a single bound to fulfill the expectations. And if such a person existed, why would they want to settle for the ordinary person who made the list?

At the other extreme, some people believe that if you are a Christian, it doesn't matter who you date or marry because of God's grace and blessings. In Psalm 37:23, however, we learn that "The steps of a good man are ordered by the Lord, and He delights in his way." That certainly sounds as if the Lord cares and has a plan for each of us. Further, Genesis 2:22 tells us that God "...brought her to the man." He was actively involved in creating the union between husband and wife. I believe God intervenes in our lives (sometimes with angelic assistance, as with Isaac and Rebekah) and takes the initiative in bringing the right people together. If God is leading you to the gift of marriage, He has someone picked out for you and is preparing him or her for you.

Begin praying now for your mate, even if you have not yet met—even if you have not started dating at all. Praying for someone before you meet begins the process of establishing your relationship in the Lord.

Q. How can I be sure he (or she) is the one?
A. I suggest making a Compatibility Checklist. This is not an empty list of physical attributes, minimum educational requirements, or income guidelines, but an insightful inventory of the qualities you want in a date and, eventually, in a mate.

Looking at dating from a Christian standpoint is vastly different from the way the world regards dating. Some might even feel that this cautious approach is too legalistic and serious for something as lighthearted as dating.

I would encourage anyone feeling this way to talk with

people who have entered into dating and marriage lightly and are now in marriages that lack peace and contentment. Ask them if it would have been worth the effort of praying in earnest and seeking God's will in finding the right person.

Compatibility Checklist

1. Physical Attraction

Again, this is not a list of arbitrary physical standards but a commitment to finding a mate who is attractive to you. When you consider physical beauty, remember, this is one area that is *guaranteed* to eventually change. We are all subject to the effects of aging, and while it's very important to be physically attracted to one another, physical beauty may be the least reliable of the qualities we seek. Proverbs 31:30 reminds us that "Charm is deceitful and beauty is passing, but a woman who fears the Lord, she shall be praised." This goes for men as well because we are also subject to thinning hair and thickening profiles.

2. Emotional Compatibility

It's a wonderful feeling to be needed by someone. But during the dating phase, strive to look at the person who needs you or whom you need with the long-term in mind. Is the need really an unhealthy dependence? Is it a situation of "I need, therefore I love," or is it "I love, therefore I need?"

Make sure you spend a great deal of time in groups. A setting with many people and personalities offers an opportunity to learn a great deal about each other. Is your date positive, kind, funny, compassionate? When embarrassed, does he or she handle it gracefully? Is there a tendency to be jealous or petty? This is the time to watch and learn his/her responses to life.

What about family values? I've heard it said that if you want to see the true person, watch him or her relate to any siblings. I believe the important point is to be with each other in family situations; get an idea of the influences and attitudes that shaped each of you. Talk about your own family goals— not just, "I want a boy and a girl," but discuss the kind of atmosphere you want in your family and home.

How does your date handle anger, rejection, and fear? Are you often relieved when your date is over because you've had to deal with these taxing emotions? Take note of these situations and your feelings—they are important and revealing glimpses into your overall emotional compatibility.

3. Spiritual Compatibility

Is the individual you're dating a representative of Jesus Christ? Does he or she have a high spiritual outlook? If you are a female, is your guy a spiritual leader? Does he have spiritual priorities? If you marry him, he will be the spiritual leader. Is he ready for that? And guys, is she a woman after God's heart? Will she be a godly mother to your children?

In my own dating experience, my wife and I were attracted to each other and emotionally compatible, but at first the spiritual compatibility was not what it should have been. After eight months, we broke up. A year and a half later, we decided to resume dating. We went out to dinner, and when I saw that she knew the Lord in such a beautiful way, I fell in love with her spiritually. With that vital spiritual element in place, our relationship had the stability it lacked earlier. We prayed that night and when we said goodbye, I walked away feeling so edified, so uplifted—it was great!

Christians who date have a great advantage over non-Christians. You don't have to worry about "breaking the ice" because you have Christ as common ground. Pray with that person. You learn so much by listening to someone pray to his/her heavenly Father.

Before my wife and I were married, we witnessed to-gether. As a team, we each shared our individual stories while the other one was quietly supportive. It was a great experience that I highly recommend to dating couples. Even if nothing develops from your relationship, what have you lost if you date this way? You have simply glorified God and helped prepare each other for your future spouses.

4. Test Your Relationship before the Lord

Communicate your feelings as you date. Don't make hasty decisions, just watch, observe, and trust the Lord. Remember, there are countless people who would like the opportunity to rethink and test their relationships before com-mitting to marriage.

During our engagement, we had some rocky times. Although we were planning the wedding, I, "Mr. No-Commitment Skip," was thinking, "I don't know if we really should do this...." It was during this period that I received a letter from my future bride which said, "Skip, I love you so much that if I am not God's highest for your life, I do not want to marry you."

That completely blew me away! I would have expected her letter to read, "I love you so much, I can't let you go!" But her love was not selfish, it was selfless. That is Christian love.

Keep in mind that God wants the best for you. Contrary to what some people think, a life lived for God is an exciting adventure. Jesus said, "...I have come that they may have life, and that they may have it more abundantly" (John 10:10b). If you are single and feeling forgotten by God, remember that He has a plan just for you and wants you to live life to the fullest within that plan.

Dating can be a time of joy and excitement, as well as a time of careful, godly reflection. Bring Christ's love and guidance into your dating relationship, and together you will be winners in the dating game.

Chapter Four

Tying the Marriage Knot: The Original Blueprint

Marriage—The Master's Plan

On the evening I proposed to my wife, I drove to her house with every intention of asking her to marry me. After an hour, however, I still hadn't popped the question. Instead, I beat around the bush using lengthy analogies, while she just stared at me, baffled. When I *finally* asked the question, I was in such a state of shock that when she said yes, I didn't even hear her. We were silent for a moment, and she repeated, "I said yes." When it dawned on me what she had said, I stood up and stammered, "You said yes? Now wait—wait—let's not be too hasty! I'm going to get a drink of water, and when I come back we gotta talk about this."

Marriage is indeed a big commitment which should not be entered into lightly. One who is approaching this turn in the road should slow down and proceed cautiously because it is intended to be a life-long commitment. Someone once said that marriage is like a violin—it doesn't work without strings, and when the music stops, the strings are still attached. I guess that's what made me so petrified—a lifetime can last a long time!

I vividly remember our wedding. It was outdoors on a beautiful June day in southern California. In addition to being shaky and nervous, the tuxedo shop had given me shoes that were a size and a half too small, so I was miserable. The tension of the monumental occasion, the summer heat, and my cramped toes left me feeling overwhelmed. But when the moment of truth arrived, and I looked back and watched my bride walk down the aisle toward me, all my fear and discomfort faded away. When she was finally by my side, all I could say to her was, "Wow!" (California surf-lingo for "God, thank You for this awesome gift!)

The Need for a Plan

It's a beautiful thing when God brings a woman to a man. One of the joys of my ministry is performing weddings. Sadly, I also see many marriages end in divorce. It breaks my heart to see couples divorce who I felt certain understood the marriage commitment and God's regard for it. As a pastor, I frequently receive letters that express the despair of a dying relationship:

> How does a woman pretend everything is okay with her mate when actually everything is falling apart? My desire for his conversation, fellowship, and intimacy is leaving.

Unfortunately, this woman is not alone in her disillusionment; she is part of a growing number of people who are just going through the motions of marriage. Like the violin, the music has stopped, but the strings are still attached. Keep in mind that these letters did not come from unbelievers but from the churchgoing mainstream. In another letter, a man shares the pain of being in a marriage that is no longer functioning:

> I do not want to go back to this woman because I feel like I don't love her anymore. I know God does

not believe in divorce, but I don't want to make her miserable, and I don't want her to make me miserable anymore.

In courtrooms across the nation, the gavel echoes the final decree of "divorce granted" hundreds of times a day. A recent poll taken by a family magazine reported that a whopping 71 percent of those surveyed said they believed the American family was in trouble. In another survey, 75 percent of the married couples polled said they believed their own marriages were failures and their homes were unhappy. In yet another survey, young married couples between the ages of twenty and thirty-five revealed that only six couples out of 100 felt their marriages were fulfilling. That's only one sixteenth of the population!

These sobering statistics can deflate anyone who dreams of wedded bliss. So, let's take a good look at what the inventor of marriage intended when He cooked up the idea. As we do, remember, even if marriages are made in heaven, we humans are responsible for their maintenance.

God's Model Home

The first Scriptural mention of marriage is in the book of beginnings: Genesis. This is God's model home; the premise upon which God brought man and woman together. When studying math or science, we learn that the premise dictates how that problem is solved. If we begin with a faulty premise, we will arrive at a faulty solution. Conversely, a correct premise allows a correct result. Genesis 2 is the premise and foundation of marriage and home.

Medicines have labels which caution us to follow the instructions for the best results. This is good advice for relieving a simple physical ailment, so just think how much more we need to follow the instructions God provided in the Bible for keeping our marriages healthy and loving:

And the Lord God said, "It is not good that man should be alone; I will make him a helper comparable to him." Out of the ground the Lord God formed every beast of the field and every bird of the air, and brought them to Adam to see what he would call them. And whatever Adam called each living creature, that was its name. So Adam gave names to all cattle, to the birds of the air, and to every beast of the field. But for Adam there was not found a helper comparable to him. And the Lord God caused a deep sleep to fall on Adam, and he slept; and He took one of his ribs, and closed up the flesh in its place. Then the rib which the Lord God had taken from man He made into a woman, and He brought her to the man. And Adam said: "This is now bone of my bones and flesh of my flesh; she shall be called Woman, because she was taken out of Man." Therefore a man shall leave his father and mother and be joined to his wife, and they shall become one flesh. And they were both naked, the man and his wife, and were not ashamed. (Gen. 2:18-25)

The words "leave father and mother and be joined to his wife" denote a public demonstration of a man and a woman coming together. I have been asked, "Why do we need to have a church wedding, stand before a preacher, and sign a paper? Isn't it good enough to stand under a tree out in the woods and say our vows to one another before God?" No, it's not good enough. Marriage involves a public commitment. It's a cop-out to try to replace wedding vows with a moment of silent prayer!

A Matter for Heavenly Jurisdiction

Thankfully, marriage was God's idea. Because it's His

design, He has a divine purpose and a written revelation, or plan, to show us how it should work.

Just imagine what marriage would be like if man had come up with the idea. He may have reasoned, "Maybe I'll get married—it's a great tax shelter and a good way to have legitimate children." Pretty romantic! But many people view this holy institution as little more than a human experiment. It's as though the marriage vows have been changed from "until death do us part" to "until something better comes along."

A comic strip reflected this modern view of marriage. One character said, "You know, it's odd, but now that I'm actually engaged I'm starting to feel nervous about marriage!" The other character replied, "It's only natural to be nervous. Marriage is a big commitment—seven or eight years can be a long time!"

If marriage had been invented by man, we would have every right to regulate it or even to dismiss it altogether. The state, for instance, would be entitled to grant a divorce on the basis of mutual incompatibility or for any other reason. But marriage was God's idea, not ours. Therefore the Scripture, not the state, has jurisdiction over it. We are not entitled to manipulate marriage by our personal whims, nor are we to violate it by blatantly behaving contrary to the written revelation of God. Some may cloak their disobedience by saying, "My wife and I don't get along, and I feel God is leading me to leave her and marry someone else." In such cases, one thing is certain: "...Indeed, let God be true but every man a liar" (Rom. 3:4). God would never lead or prompt anyone to break His commands. Our whims do not regulate an institution God has created.

Now, I realize that I'm headed for turbulent waters with this topic. Marriage, divorce, and remarriage are hot-potato issues which can inspire controversy and disagreement.

While it is our individual prerogative to disagree, we need to realize that deviation from God's way hurts not only ourselves but the whole Body of Christ. The truths of God can both comfort the afflicted and afflict the comfortable. We must decide to rest our case with the Scripture rather than our opinions.

Adam's Almost Perfect World

In the garden of Eden, Adam had it made! He lived in a paradise with a perfect ecological system, a beautiful environment free of hassles, mortgages, taxes, faxes, smog, and traffic. He had one of the most interesting and creative jobs imaginable: He observed and named the animals. In addition to all of this, he had close fellowship with the Creator. What a life! A very good life.

After every episode of creation, God affirmed the rightness of His work. The earth yielded grass and seed, the trees bore abundant fruit, and it was good. The sun, moon, and stars were placed in the heavens. God made the creatures of the sea, the air, and all the creatures on the land, and "Then God saw everything that He had made, and indeed it was very good...." (Gen. 1:31).

Man's First Problem and God's Solution

In stark contrast to God's affirmation of the goodness of the creation process, there was still a problem in paradise—man's aloneness:

> *And the Lord God said, "It is not good that man should be alone; I will make him a helper comparable to him." (Gen. 2:18)*

By himself, man was missing something, and the missing ingredient was a woman. She was a different kind of person from the man, and she was to be the object of his devotion. As Edmund Burke put it, "Woman was not made to be the admiration of all but the happiness of one."

God created male and female different from one another. He did not create male and male, female and female, nor two unisex creatures. It was God's intention to bring together these two uniquely different creatures:

Then God said, "Let Us make man in Our image, according to Our likeness; let them have dominion over the fish of the sea, over the birds of the air, and over the cattle, over all the earth and over every creeping thing that creeps on the earth." So God created man in His own image; in the image of God He created him; male and female He created them. (Gen. 1:26-27)

Similarly, marriage was designed by God to unite man and woman and solve this first and fundamental problem of humanity—loneliness. He cared about Adam's aloneness and responded to it by making him a helper. God didn't figure that because *most* of Adam's needs were met, He would disregard his loneliness. He set about to remedy Adam's problem by preparing a perfect mate.

Now, think about it. Would God do less for His children today? I often hear people say that they have decided to go out with unbelievers because they can't find Christians to date. That's a slap in the face to the Creator who is preparing a mate for you just as He did for Adam.

Eve was both a mate and a helper for Adam. On the surface, *helper* sounds as though the wife is a subordinate part of the husband's work team rather than a cherished partner. Misinterpreting this verse has led some men to behave as though they had made this kind of wedding vow to their wives: "From this day forward, I take you to be my lawfully wedded cook, to clean and to fold, until death do *you* part."

This is not much of an improvement from the ancient Hebrews and Greeks who regarded women as subordinate, convenient necessities.

God never intended woman to be inferior or subordinate. He envisioned woman as a helper and companion to man. Some of the varied translations of Genesis 2:18 show woman as man's counterpart, other half, partner, correspondent; someone of his own kind who is especially suited to him.

From Rib to Woman

God created woman by using part of His original creation. He put Adam under divine anesthesia and performed His delicate operation:

> *And the Lord God caused a deep sleep to fall on Adam, and he slept; and He took one of his ribs, and closed up the flesh in its place. Then the rib which the Lord God had taken from man He made into a woman, and He brought her to the man. (Gen. 2:21-22)*

It's significant that God made woman from the rib of man. There's a saying that expounds on this fact:

Woman was not taken from man's head
Lest she should rule over him;
Woman was not taken from man's feet
 Lest he should dominate her; but
Woman was taken from man's side
To be close to his heart,
Next to his side,
To signify that she was to be as dear unto him
As his own flesh...

God intended woman to be her husband's helper—to be by his side and in his heart. The husband protects his wife, and the wife, in turn, protects her family. C.S. Lewis spoke of the protective nature of women by aptly comparing it to the rib cage which protects the vital organs. He further illustrated this protective nature when he said, "If the neighbor's child was bitten by your dog, would you rather face the father or the mother in discussing the issue?"

God's idea was to create a comparable partner who would help Adam reach fulfillment. The word *helper* is the same Hebrew word used in Psalm 46 to describe God as "a very present *help* in trouble." The image conveys woman as a helper and companion who will rescue man from his loneliness.

God did not just provide a generic wife for Adam. He knew Adam's unique needs, and He fashioned Eve to be his perfect counterpart. Today, when God brings two people together, regardless of their differences and backgrounds, they are "built" for each other by God in the very same way.

At Last—Completion

Adam must have had a growing sense of excitement as his wedding day approached. He was God's first human creation, he lived in the ultimate environment and was directly cared for by God. What could be better? Adam found out when God brought Eve to him. And he didn't take it lightly:

And Adam said: "This is now bone of my bones and flesh of my flesh; she shall be called Woman because she was taken out of Man." Therefore a man shall leave his father and mother and be joined to his wife, and they shall become one flesh. And they were both naked, the man and his wife, and were not ashamed. (Gen. 2:23-25)

Now, that seems like a rather odd response from a man about his bride. Today, it's hard to imagine a groom whispering to his best man, "Look! Bone of my bones and flesh of my flesh is coming down the aisle!" But the feeling behind this statement was sheer excitement—something like, "At last, my completion! This is what I've been waiting for—the one who will compliment my life!" Adam was filled with joy when God brought him a wife. Most men *still* feel this way on their wedding day.

The joy of the wedding day should last throughout the marriage. The emotions may not be exactly the same, but the joy of relationship should be. I believe that God can hand-pick a mate for us, and He *delights* in doing so. A Christian should not marry just anyone he or she may capriciously choose. Instead, the relationship should be tested carefully and prayerfully with the realization that it is God who brings the two together.

For those who are already married in the Lord, do you remember the time when you were certain you should marry your wife or husband? You *knew* that God brought the two of you together. Stop right now, and recall that time. Have you lost touch with those feelings? Has your commitment to your spouse waned over the years? Remember that the Lord Himself saw that it was not good for you to be alone, and He brought you and your wife together with the same care He used to bring Adam and Eve together. Don't allow your marriage to become a casualty statistic. For many, marriage is like flies on a screen door; those on the outside want in, but some of those on the inside want out. Reject that trend!

When I perform a wedding, I have the best seat in the house. The bride and groom are only a foot away from me, and I can watch their faces and their electric interaction. Recently, at a wedding ceremony I performed, when the groom saw his bride coming down the aisle, his expression and his body language were almost shouting, "She is mine!" Adam's response to Eve was similar. He knew Eve was given to rescue and complete him. What a change it could make in your marriage if your wife or husband knew you felt the same way.

Joined in Wedded Freedom

Bachelors sometimes mourn the prospect of losing their freedom. They have elaborate bachelor parties and grieve over forsaking independence for the shackled life of matrimony. Bunk! That couldn't be further from God's intention. The wedding day is really their first day of freedom. In the union of marriage, man is released to reach complete and utter fulfillment—to become all God intended him to be.

For both women and men, a new dimension is added to life. Now there is someone with whom hopes, ambitions, dreams, fears, and love can be shared. In this secure atmosphere, the couple's most intimate thoughts can be voiced. As Howard Hendricks put it, "Marriage is not finding the person with whom you can live but finding the person you cannot live without."

A little girl had just heard the story of *Snow White* for the first time. She could scarcely contain herself until she told her mother all about it. After telling how Prince Charming had arrived on his beautiful white horse and kissed Snow White back to life, she asked her mother, "And do you know what happened then?"

"Yes," said her mom, "they lived happily ever after."

"No," responded Suzie, with a frown, "they got married."

It doesn't have to be that way! Our Creator meant for married life to be freeing, fulfilling, and happy. I can attest to the fact that the wife enables her husband to develop and reach his full potential. My wife has done for me what no other human being has been able to do. She has brought dimension to my life, expanded my horizons, and balanced me in many areas. As God intended, she completes me and has brought me to fulfillment.

The Gift and the Responsibility

One Sunday, I suggested that the people in the congregation hug the person next to them. After the service, I was handed an anonymous note which graphically illustrated the consequences of neglected responsibility:

> Dear Skip,
> My husband did as you suggested and hugged the person next to him. We sleep in the same bed, and until that hug this morning, we have had no physical contact in three months.

In those few lines, her pain is palpable. The person who was meant to nurture and tend to her seemed like a stranger.

The ability to complete the life of a spouse is a tremendous gift which carries with it an equally tremendous responsibility. God's plan is that we reach physical, emotional, intellectual, and spiritual fulfillment with our mates. Therefore, to the degree to which we are not meeting the needs of our mate, our mate is alone. Loneliness, therefore, is certainly not confined to single people. In fact, last night, the loneliest person in your zip code may have been a married person sitting on the edge of his or her bed praying, "God, will it ever get better? Will our love ever be rekindled?" It is not good for man to be alone—*especially* in marriage.

Three Principles of Marital Success

Marriage counseling has become a pervasive fixture in our modern society. Couples attend expensive sessions for months and even years—sometimes without success. The best marriage counseling ever given was also the most concise. After God brought the first couple together, He said to Adam, the newlywed:

Therefore a man shall leave his father and mother and be joined to his wife, and the two shall become one flesh. And they were both naked, the man and his wife, and were not ashamed. (Gen. 2:24-25)

This passage, distilled to its essence, conveys the three principles for a successful marriage: *leaving* father and mother, *cleaving* (being joined) to each other, and *becoming one flesh*. Let's examine each principle.

Leaving: The First Principle

God's first counsel to Adam was to leave father and mother. This is especially interesting since Adam had neither! God gave this as a principle for mankind. Marriage must begin with leaving other life-long relationships so that the new union between husband and wife can solidify.

The relationship with mom and dad is normally the closest one outside of marriage and is primarily based on dependency. Mom and dad have been the source of money, encouragement, and home. Leaving father and mother does not mean abandoning them. Nor does it mean never calling them or listening to their advice once the marriage license has been signed. It means that now we lean on our spouse rather than on them. God directed this instruction primarily to the man because he is meant to take the spiritual initiative and leadership in his home.

Before I perform a wedding, I ask the couple how their parents feel about the marriage. I get a variety of answers such as, "Oh, they're very excited. In fact they're paying for everything, and they made all the wedding plans. They even bought us a home!" Or sometimes the parents don't approve: "My mom says I shouldn't marry him. She thinks he's a creep." Either of these responses can cause strain in the marriage. The most generous and well-meaning financial assistance may make it difficult to separate from the parents because the couple feels indebted. If the parents are against the relationship, the first time the new couple has a fight, the bride may go home to her mom where she will hear, "Didn't I tell you this would happen? You never should have married him." This only hinders the solution to the problem.

One of the greatest gifts parents can give their child on the wedding day is to *release* him or her to the new mate. I believe this is something the parents should verbalize. In doing so, both they and the new couple have taken an important step toward respecting and nurturing the union.

During our first year of marriage, we often called my wife's father who, on occasion, graciously offered advice. He would always carefully add, "Now, honey, Skip is the head of your family. This is just an idea. If he doesn't go along with it, scrap it." His respect for our marriage allowed us to consider his suggestions objectively.

Leaving can go beyond the need to cut the cord of dependency with parents. It stands to reason that if the close relationship with parents must, in a sense, be broken, lesser ties must be reprioritized as well. Sometimes these ties are harder to identify: hobbies, friends, church work, or television can rob the couple of much-needed time together.

Ironically, one of the greatest curses plaguing the ministry is the belief that the needs of the church come before the pastor's marriage. They absolutely don't! A minister's first priority is his relationship to God. Second is his relationship to his wife and children, and third (and never out of this order) is the responsibility to the church. The best gift a pastor can give to his congregation is to love his wife.

Another danger can arise when the couple starts a family. Children can subtly begin to take first place in the family, pushing the husband/wife relationship to the background. Although parents want to spend time nurturing and loving their children, they must be secondary to the husband and wife. Rightly ordering family relationships ensures a stable home and secure children.

There is a law in science called the second law of thermo-dynamics. This law states that any closed system left to itself tends toward greater randomness; that is, it breaks down. It is a fixed law that it takes an ordered input of energy to keep anything together. This can be illustrated in home mainte-nance. To keep a house in good repair, time and energy must be invested on a daily, monthly, and yearly basis.

The second law of thermodynamics also applies to the marriage relationship. Marriage must have a daily, monthly, and yearly investment of time and energy to be enjoyable. If no energy is expended, the relationship will eventually need a complete overhaul, or it will be knocked down. A wise couple will continually build their marriage rather than passively wait until a complete overhaul is needed—either in the counselor's office or the courtroom.

Cleaving: The Second Principle

In Genesis 2, we read that a man shall be *joined* to his wife. The Hebrew word for *joined* or *cleave* is *dabaq* which means "to be glued or cemented together." When God glues people together in marriage, it is meant to be a permanent bond. When a marriage breaks up, what remains are not two people but fractions of one. If we glued together two pieces of paper, when the glue dried, the pieces would be bonded into one solid unit. It would be impossible to separate what had been joined without causing great damage to both pieces of paper. Similarly, the bond of marriage simply cannot be broken without great damage.

People often enter into marriage with a "loophole" men-tality, thinking there is always the alternative of divorce if the marriage gets too tough. With that thought lingering in the back of their minds, it's not surprising that when troubles appear, thoughts of divorce creep from the back of their minds to the front.

Wedding vows should be regarded as eternal promises. When performing a wedding ceremony, I look the groom in the eye when I ask, "Will you have this woman to be your lawfully wedded, God-given wife? Will you love her, honor her, and forsaking all others, cleave only unto her for as long as you both shall live?" I appreciate it when a man thinks about it before answering, "I will."

Promises made without meaning or passion are empty formalities. This was the case with a couple I know who wrote and signed a marriage contract before their wedding. The contract detailed their expectations and provided a way out of the marriage if either broke the contract. Their marriage lasted four months. The most iron-clad contract can not create the gluing or cleaving God designed for life-long marriage. It is sad when couples bring shallow expectations and superficial commitments into a marriage:

When I got married,
I was looking for an ideal.
Then it became an ordeal.
Now I want a new deal.

Cleaving to one another is a process that begins with the wedding and strengthens throughout the marriage. Leaving a marriage should not be regarded as simply tearing down the old to make way for the new.

The structure of the stage I stand on illustrates the complex process of cleaving. The stage was built in phases using metal strips and braces. Layer by layer, the builders welded sections together at strategic points to make it solid and firm. If the sections had not been joined together, the result would have been a shaky stage. So it is when forming the ties of marriage. It takes effort, care, and guidance from God, the expert builder.

Becoming One Flesh: The Third Principle

Commitment sets the stage for the third, and final, principle for marital success—oneness and intimacy:

Therefore a man shall leave his father and mother and be joined to his wife, and they shall become one flesh. And they were both naked, the man and his wife, and were not ashamed. (Gen. 2:24-25)

Becoming one flesh does not instantaneously occur when the minister says, "I now pronounce you man and wife." It is a life-long process of becoming and growing together. Adjusting to each other's quirks and habits is no easy task, but when our marriages are surrounded by commitment, we are incredibly enriched.

Marriage has been likened to two porcupines on a cold winter night. When the icy wind blows against them, they move closer together. However, when close, they stick one another with their quills. If they move apart, they are cold once again. In order to keep warm, they must learn to adjust cautiously as they move close. Although we *need* each other, like porcupines we sometimes *needle* each other in the process!

Utmost care must be taken as we "become one." All too often, love degenerates rather than generates. Instead of adjusting to each other's quills, couples sometimes refuse to adjust to differences, and they drift apart.

Some time ago, the *Saturday Evening Post* ran an article that illustrated this tendency. Entitled "The Seven Ages of the Married Cold," the article tracked a husband's reaction to his wife's colds during the first seven years of marriage:

The first year: "Sugar dumpling, I'm worried about my baby girl. You've got a bad sniffle, and there's no telling about these things with all this strep around. I'm putting you in the hospital this afternoon for a general checkup and a good rest. I know the food's lousy, but I'll bring your meals in from Rossini's. I've already got it arranged with the floor superintendent."

The second year: "Listen, darling, I don't like the sound of that cough. I've called Doc Miller to rush over here. Now, you go to bed like a good girl, please? Just for Papa."

The third year: "Maybe you'd better lie down, honey; nothing like a little rest when you're feeling punk. I'll bring you something to eat. Have we got any soup?"

The fourth year: "Look, dear, be sensible. After you feed the kids and get the dishes washed, you'd better hit the sack."

The fifth year: "Why don't you get yourself a couple of aspirin?"

The sixth year: "Why don't you gargle or something, rather than sitting around barking like a seal!"

The seventh year: "For Pete's sake, stop sneezing! What are you trying to do, give me pneumonia?"

For Adam and Eve, "becoming one" enabled them to be naked and unashamed. This refers both to sexual togetherness and total, uninhibited openness. This is the intimacy which allows a man to share his fears without being rejected and makes a woman feel secure and trusting of her husband.

The openness continued for the first couple until Genesis 3 when sin entered their lives. At that point, they became selfish and were self-consciously aware of their nakedness, saying, "God, we're naked!"

Struggling in Your Marriage? Go Back to God's Plan

Why is it hard for husbands and wives to relate to each other and have satisfying, intimate relationships? Why are so many marriages struggling, and why are so many failing? It may be that one or both partners have not totally left other distracting relationships or passions. Perhaps the couple has never submitted to the process of cleaving or being cemented together. Whatever the reason, they have surely left the Master's plan, created for a satisfying marriage.

Sometimes at weddings, I read a portion of a letter written in the 1920s by Dr. James Dobson's father to his fiancé before they walked down the aisle. It reflects a high view of marriage and a beautiful commitment:

> I want you to understand and be fully aware of my feelings concerning the marriage covenant which we are about to enter. I have been taught on my mother's knee, and in harmony with the Word of God, that the marriage vows are inviolable, and by entering into them, I am binding myself absolutely and for life. The idea of estrangement from you through divorce for any reason at all, although God allows infidelity, will never, at any time, be permitted to enter into my thinking. I am not naive in this. On the contrary, I am fully aware of the possibility. Unlikely as it now appears that mutual incompatibility or other unforeseen circumstances could result in extreme mental suffering, if such becomes the case, I am resolved from my part to accept it as a consequence of the commitment I am now making and to bear it if necessary to the end of our lives together. I have loved you dearly as a sweetheart and will continue to love you as my wife. But over and above that, I love you with a Christian love that demands that I never react

in any way toward you that would jeopardize our prospects of entering heaven, which is the supreme objective of both of our lives. I pray that God Himself will make our affection for one another perfect and eternal.

Now that's a love letter! It depicts the essence of a term that has become a dirty word in our society: commitment. When a marriage is enveloped in commitment, God's marriage pattern works beautifully. The wedding vows are not just quaint, traditional phrases; they depict the devotion and commitment that are necessary to make marriage work: "...for better or for worse, for richer or for poorer, in sickness and in health, till death do us part."

In this complex world, it is sometimes difficult to return to the fundamentals. Don't be deceived. While God's plan is simple, it is also profound. Regardless of the problems in your marriage, they are not too big for God. Take your marriage to the Master Weaver and let Him guide you through the process of reweaving the loose threads of your relationship based on *His* principles. My prayer for you is that He will enter into your relationship and make it perfect and eternal.

Chapter Five

A Rope Firmly Secured: Relational Rules in Marriage

Getting What You Expected?

In counseling sessions, marital problems are addressed more frequently than all other problems combined. Among marriage-oriented concerns, understanding the roles of the husband/wife relationship are among the most common.

Do the following stereotypes sound familiar? The husband fixes the car, cleans up after the dog, takes out the garbage, and mows the lawn. The wife cleans and decorates the house, irons, cooks, and takes care of the children. Although these might not represent your personal feelings, we all harbor stereotypes of what we think the roles of the marriage relationship should be. We enter marriage with certain expectations, and we assume our mate will fulfill those expectations. Many times we never verbalize our expectations until our ideals collide with reality as in the following imagined scenarios:

What She Expects:
1. Her husband will be a brilliant conversationalist.
2. He will be sensitive, kind, understanding, and loving.

3. He will work hard.
4. He'll help around the house, wash dishes, vacuum the floor, and care for the yard.
5. He will help raise the children and will be a great father.
6. He will be physically and emotionally strong.
7. He will be as smart as Albert Einstein and look like Robert Redford.

What She Gets:
1. He's so dull, she's bored even when he's giving her a compliment.
2. He doesn't have any ulcers; he's too busy giving them.
3. He's well-known as a miracle worker—it's a miracle when he works.
4. He helps her with dinner by taking her out to eat. Some day he may even take her *inside* the restaurant instead of to the drive-up window.
5. Occasional flashes of silence make his conversation brilliant.
6. Whenever he has an idea, the whole thing could fit in a nutshell.
7. He has the looks of Albert Einstein and the brains of Robert Redford.

What He Expects:
1. She will be a stimulating conversationalist.
2. She insists that doing the yard work keeps her figure looking like a model's.
3. She's a natural beauty without the help of curlers or beauty shops.
4. She will be an expert cook and homemaker.
5. Her favorite expression will be, "What can I do for you, dear?"
6. She will think everything he says and does is brilliant.
7. She'll hate charge cards.

What He Gets:
1. She speaks 140 words a minute with gusts up to 180.
2. She was once a model—for a totem pole.
3. No matter what she does with her hair, it looks like an explosion in a steel wool factory.
4. She is a light eater: as soon as it's light, she starts eating.
5. Where there's smoke—she's probably there cooking.
6. She thinks he has only two faults—everything he says and everything he does.
7. If she gets lost, he just opens his wallet, and she magically appears.

You may be smiling right now, but there is an ounce or two of truth to these fictional expectations. After the first year or so of marriage, we may wonder what happened to that romantic dream-person we thought we married. In reality, failed expectations often result in pain, despair, and heartbreak as shown in the following letter written to me a few years ago:

> How does a wife with three preschoolers keep a smile on her face and a song in her heart when her husband is always creating depressing conditions in the home? He spends more than he makes on things for himself rather than for the family. He sleeps too much. He watches TV all day long. The house needs repair—the yard and garage are in a shambles. The washing machine doesn't work. We eat too many beans and noodles and not enough meat. I'm home all day with no gas and not enough food. I'm bored and exhausted trying to keep up with the house and the kids. I'm becoming bitter.

Disappointment and worry are not confined to wives. One husband wrote and admitted his patience was paper-thin:

She has no respect for the head of the home. She rebels and thinks that her way of doing things is always the right way. She never submits to what is right in God's eyes. She never listens when I try to share a simple passage. I try my very best to love my wife as the Bible says, but I'm going on the 9,000th mile with her. Pray for me that I may be faithful to the Lord and that I may walk a perfect life before her so the put-downs and the persecutions will stop. I'm exhausted putting up with her slander. At times, I feel like packing my bags and leaving for good, but I know it's wrong because the Bible has clearly spoken on divorce.

From these pain-filled letters, we see how marriages can go dreadfully awry. It's time we Christians declare *God's* standard for our marriages; not what *we* think marriage should be like but what the Bible says. In doing so, we will discover God's plan for fulfilling marriages.

It Started in the Garden

When Eve sinned in the garden of Eden, she not only disobeyed God, she usurped her husband's authority by acting independently. Adam sinned by passively nodding to Eve's sinful decision rather than assuming leadership and responsibility. In doing so, he not only disobeyed God, he forfeited his God-given authority as head of the family unit. This single, monumental act of sin brought about a reversal of the husband and wife roles, resulting in a downward spiral which has left the family unit near collapse.

We have become complacent about sin and its effects on marriage and the family. In the 1960s and 1970s, we were shocked when couples lived together outside of marriage—now it seems normal and reasonable. After all, what better way to make sure this is the right person? One pastor of a large, evangelical church said that 70 percent of the couples he counsels prior to marriage have been living together.

Gays and lesbians are demanding the right to marry, and the government and some churches agree. Family situations can become terribly convoluted as gays leave their heterosexual relationships. Their children must struggle with both the marriage breakup and the confusion of being brought into the parent's new gay marriage where they are told that it, too, is a normal family. Was this really what God had in mind for families and marriages?

Husbands and Wives: The God-Intended Roles

In His wisdom, God made the roles of husband and wife simple and straightforward. By simple, I don't mean easy. Anyone who is married knows better. But God didn't make a lengthy list of duties for husbands and wives to perform. He put forth a few basic principles that are far more encompassing than simply taking out the trash or cleaning the house!

The Apostle Paul gives us these principles in his letter to the Ephesians. In his letter, Paul made the assumption that both husband and wife were believers who were submitted to God and leading Spirit-controlled lives. This is an important consideration because, ironically, the roles for husbands and wives described in the following passages won't work well *unless* the individuals are first submitted to God. When unbelievers (or for that matter, carnal believers) attempt to apply these principles in their marriages, we tend to see the abuse and domination that have caused women to rebel against the concept of submission. The Bible reminds us that our efforts apart from Him are fruitless, because unless the Lord builds the house, they labor in vain who try and build it. To make marriage work smoothly, the husband and wife must be individually submitted to God and to one another.

93

And do not be drunk with wine, in which is dissipation; but be filled with the Spirit, speaking to one another in psalms and hymns and spiritual songs, singing and making melody in your heart to the Lord, giving thanks always for all things to God the Father in the name of our Lord Jesus Christ, submitting to one another in the fear of God. Wives, submit to your own husbands, as to the Lord. For the husband is head of the wife, as also Christ is head of the church; and He is the Savior of the body. Therefore, just as the church is subject to Christ, so let the wives be to their own husbands in everything. (Eph. 5:18-24)

Submission can be a prickly issue today. Some people consider it politically incorrect or intolerable. In relationships of all kinds—whether with husband, wife, friend, or relative—when a need is recognized, our response as believers should be deference to meeting that need. In this respect, submission is an equally important word for both women and men.

In its literal translation, *submission* means "to arrange in a ranking file, as in an infantry." In its practical application, a submissive attitude results in a team-player mentality that is more concerned with seeing the team win than with fulfilling individual desires. *The Saturday Evening Post* printed an article about Coach Lou Holtz of Notre Dame's Fighting Irish that reflects this winning principle:

> "When it comes to discipline here," Holtz says, "we ask three questions: Will it make him a better man? A better student? A better athlete? If the answer is yes, we make him do it. The next step is up to him. An individual has a choice when you discipline him: either to become bitter or better."

Judging by his squad's record, Lou Holtz's discipline has resulted in better men. So, too, a husband and wife must submit to the disciplines that would make their marriage-team great.

Submission Does Not Mean Women Are Inferior to Men

We would be heretics if we called Jesus Christ inferior, yet He functioned in total submission to the Father. He poured out His life, and in John 6:38 He said, "For I have come down from heaven, not to do My own will, but the will of Him who sent Me." Jesus was in complete and voluntary submission to His Father. In the garden of Gethsemane He said, "...O My Father, if it is possible, let this cup pass from Me; nevertheless, not as I will, but as You will" (Matt. 26:39). Did that mean Jesus was inferior to the Father? Of course not. Although He was equal with God, He functioned in voluntary submission to the Father. Similarly, the function of the wife is submission to her husband, but her value and worth are equal to his.

Submission Does Not Mean Husbands Should Be Dictators

Being the head does not mean the husband is a dictator. Unfortunately, there are many frustrated sergeants out there running around with biblical clubs shouting, "I'm the head of the home!" This kind of attitude causes wives to react by saying, "You may be the head of the home, but I'm the neck, and I can turn the head wherever I want." Rivalry, competition, and a manipulative relationship will result between husband and wife when both are vying for authority.

Submission Does Not Mean
Husbands Make Every Decision

Although the husband is the head of the home, that does not mean he is the always-right, executive decision-maker. He is, however, always responsible for his decisions before God. The husband should initiate but not dominate, lead but not lead blindly. And while the wife is not responsible for her husband's decisions, she is responsible for her failure to submit to him.

The Lord knows that the wife offers great insights the husband may lack. In turn, the husband can compensate for the wife's blind spots. The decision-making process becomes perfectly balanced when husband and wife are submitted to the Lord, to each other, and to their roles. It is an important act of love to take each other's feelings into consideration when a decision is made.

Somerset Maugham described his mother as lovely, charming, and admired by all. His father, however, was homely and had few social graces. Curious about this apparently mismatched relationship, someone asked his mother, "When everyone is in love with you, and you could have anyone you liked, how can you remain faithful to that ugly little man you married?" She answered simply, "He never hurts my feelings." We should never underestimate the value of being treated with tender respect.

Submission Does Not Mean Obeying Ungodly Counsel

The underlying principles of submission would be broken if a husband forbid his wife to read the Bible, go to church, be with Christian friends, or if he commanded her to do anything unbiblical. The fundamental element of a godly marriage is that both husband and wife are submitted to God. The husband's position as head of the wife does not mean he can force her to do things contrary to God's Word. In that case, she can and should oppose him because God and His commands are our first priority. Submission is a loving response to someone who loves you like Christ loves the church. A loving husband would not instruct his wife to violate God's will.

It was testimony night at a church. A lady got up and said, "We are living in a wicked land where sin always at hand. I have had a terrible fight with the old devil all week." Just then, her husband shot to his feet and said, "It's not all my fault; she's tough to get along with, too!" His response revealed his heart, wouldn't you say?

Why do you suppose Paul's first set of instructions were given to husbands? I think it's because the husband's actions set the pace for the wife's response. Much of the blame for the sorrow between the sexes must be laid at the feet of men. After sixty-nine years of life and forty-two years of marriage, Dr. Richard Halverson, Chaplin of the United States Senate, wrote:

> It is my deep, settled conviction that 100 percent of the responsibility for the sustenance of the marriage relationship belongs to the husband. The Scriptures tell us that as husbands, we need to model ourselves after Jesus Christ who gave Himself up in every way in order to present His bride to Himself without blemish, or stain, or spot, or wrinkle.

I agree. Men, let's take the first vital step to heal the brokenness of our land by submitting our lives to God and living under His lordship. Nothing is more attractive to a godly woman than a man walking tall after his God!

Wives: Submission with a Mission

Women are directed to submit to their husbands as their head, in the same manner we are subject to the Lord Jesus

Christ as head of the church:

> *Wives, submit to your own husbands, as to the Lord.*
> *For the husband is head of the wife, as also Christ is*
> *head of the church; and He is the Savior of the body.*
> *Therefore, just as the church is subject to Christ, so*
> *let the wives be to their own husbands in everything.*
> *(Eph. 5:22-24)*

The husband's position as the head does not mean he is superior or more spiritual than his wife. God has given him a function of leadership which he needs to fulfill. As it says in 1 Corinthians 11:3: "...the head of every man is Christ, the head of woman is man, and the head of Christ is God."

Wives should first be submitted to Jesus Christ. That's easy because relating and submitting to Jesus brings joy. It can be tough, however, to equate submission to a husband with submission to Christ! But if the wife refuses to submit to the husband, the root of the problem is in her relationship with the Lord.

Further, a couple's ability or inability to get along with one another serves as an example to their children. Kids are an ever-attentive audience in the home. One teenager voiced her feelings when she wrote, "I wish my parents had known that unless marriage partners truly love each other, there is little they can teach their children about the love of God or Christian living."

Submission Enables Leadership

Wives often wish their husbands would assume spiritual leadership in the home. They need to keep in mind that leadership requires that someone yields his or her power to the leader. Submission *enables* leadership and allows the husband to freely demonstrate love to his spouse.

Wives, submission to your husband as head not only demonstrates your respect for him but also your respect for the order and functions God intended in your home. Help your husband lead by handing him the reins of leadership in your home. I love the advice one pastor gave to a woman who was struggling with this:

> Madam, I think your husband is looking up-wards—making some effort to rise above the world toward God and heaven. You must not let him try alone. Whenever I see the husband struggling alone in such efforts, it makes me think of a dove endeavoring to fly upwards with one broken wing. It leaps and flutters and, perhaps, rises a little way. Then it becomes wearied and drops back again to the ground. If both wings cooperate, then it mounts easily.

Proverbs 21:29 tells us, "Wicked people are stubborn, but good people think carefully about what they do." Solomon's admonition can be applied in marriage. A stubborn refusal to submit can close the door of communication and emotional fulfillment. Loving humility, on the other hand, opens wide those doors.

Shortly after her marriage to Prince Albert, Queen Victoria had a quarrel with her new husband. Albert walked out of the room and locked himself in his private apartment. Victoria hammered furiously on the door. "Who's there?" called Albert. "The Queen of England, and she demands to be admitted." There was no response, and the door remained locked. Victoria hammered again. "Who's there?" he queried. The reply was the same, and the door remained shut. More fruitless and furious knocking was followed by a pause. Then there was a gentle tap. "Who's there?" Albert asked. "Your wife, Albert," the queen replied. The prince opened the door at once.

Was Paul a Chauvinist?

There are many people who read what Paul said about the roles of husbands and wives and conclude that Paul was either a chauvinist, or he reflected a totally patriarchal mindset. Nothing could be further from the truth. Paul wasn't down on women. In fact, the New Testament was the Declaration of Independence for women. The ancient Jews put marriage down and had such a low opinion of women they used to pray, "God, thank you that I am not a Gentile, a slave, or a woman." In the Roman world, marriage was little more than legalized prostitution. Divorce was rampant—as simple as signing a check. Seneca wrote that women were married to be divorced and divorced to be married. Jerome confirmed this by recording that in Rome there was a woman who had married her twenty-third husband, and she was his twenty-first wife! Out of these circumstances, a feminist movement arose. Women were tired of being treated so poorly, and many decided they no longer wanted to be wives or ruin their figures by having babies. Instead, they wanted to hold jobs and hunt like men.

It was in the midst of this climate that Paul came forth directing husbands to love their wives and wives to submit to their husbands as to the Lord. The atmosphere of marriage for Christians was vastly different from that of the world around them.

We must be careful of the tendency to disregard the parts of the Bible that are uncomfortable or confrontational and then to try and justify our actions. If we decide this is the only part of Scripture which is not true and inspired by God, then we have circumvented God's order. When we pick and choose what to believe from the Bible, we are paving the road to disaster. Trust that God included this information in the Bible so we would have peace and fulfillment.

Husbands: Love, Love, Love, Love

Husbands, love your wives, just as Christ also loved the church and gave Himself for her, that He might sanctify and cleanse her with the washing of water by the word, that He might present her to Himself a glorious church, not having spot or wrinkle or any such thing, but that she should be holy and without blemish. So husbands ought to love their own wives as their own bodies; he who loves his wife loves himself. For no one ever hated his own flesh, but nourishes and cherishes it, just as the Lord does the church. For we are members of His body, of His flesh and of His bones. "For this reason a man shall leave his father and mother and be joined to his wife, and the two shall become one flesh." (Eph. 5:25-31)

We all know that husbands should love their wives. However, God has given specific guidance on *how* husbands should love their wives. We will look at the four kinds of love that make up the husband's role in marriage.

1. Unconditional Love: Love without Strings

Husbands are to love their wives unconditionally, "...just as Christ also loved the church...." *The Living Bible* puts it this way: "And you husbands, show the same kind of love to your wives as Christ showed to the Church when He died for her." God's love differs greatly from the worldly "what's in it for me?" kind of love. The world's love is object-oriented; a person is loved for possessing the right positive characteristics of physical beauty, wit, charm, or other qualities deemed worthy of love. These criteria make love fickle because when those characteristics begin to fade away, love diminishes.

God's love differs radically. He doesn't love us because we're awesome, beautiful, or righteous. His nature is to love, and He made a decision to love us in spite of all of our negative characteristics. It is the same kind of committed, unconditional love Christ has for the church.

Husbands sometimes say, "But my wife has changed, and I don't feel the same." God intended us to be attracted by physical beauty; however, those characteristics will eventually fade and, with them, love, unless we decide to love without conditions. The Bible tells us that God's love is shed abroad in our hearts, and therefore we have an incredible capacity to show love unconditionally.

Remember the story of the fairy princess who kissed the toad, turning him into a prince? If you're a toad, that's great, but what if you're the princess bending down to kiss a warty old toad? God loves us although we are toads, and He loves us with unconditional love.

Husband, your wife wants to know you care for her regardless of her performance. She doesn't want love based on her cooking, how she looks, or whether she grants you sexual favors whenever you get goo-goo eyes. She wants the security and warmth of a relationship that has no strings attached.

Ann Landers once asked her women readers to reply to the question, "Would you be content to be held close and treated tenderly and forget about the [sexual] act?" She obviously struck a nerve because, within four days, the mail room was working double shifts to handle over one hundred thousand replies. Seventy-two percent of the respondents said yes, they would be content to be held close and treated tenderly, without the sexual act. Of those, 40 percent were under age forty. The obvious heart-cry of women is, "I want to be valued as a person, loved for who I am rather than for what I can give!"

2. Sacrificial Love: Love to Die for

The wife is called to live for her husband, but the husband is called to die, if necessary, for his wife. This is the kind of sacrificial love Christ had for us—He gave Himself for us. Ephesians 5:25 says, "Husbands, love your wives, just as Christ also loved the church and gave Himself for her...."

For most of us, the greatest test of sacrificial love takes place inside the four walls of home rather than in a life or death demonstration. Wouldn't a love that would lead a husband to die for his wife, also lead him to make sacrifices for her good and pleasure in countless other ways as well? This is sacrificial love. Maybe that sacrifice means *he* will clean the house once in a while or watch the children so his wife can go for coffee with her friends. There are lots of ways love can be demonstrated, but that's the point—it must be demonstrated!

In the play *My Fair Lady*, Eliza was courted by Freddy, who wrote daily to her of his love. Eliza responded to his notes by crying in frustration:

Words! Words! I'm so sick of words!
Don't talk of stars
Burning above,
If you're in love,
Show me!
Don't talk of love lasting through time,
Make me no undying vow.
Show me, now!

3. Sanctifying Love: Love with a Purpose

Christ's love has a goal. When He bought us for a price and gave Himself for us, He planned for us to be His representatives on earth and, ultimately, to be with Him forever in heaven. His non-condemning love and devotion changed, sanctified, and set us apart so that we could grow spiritually:

...that He might sanctify and cleanse her with the washing of water by the word, that He might present her to Himself a glorious church, not having spot or wrinkle or any such thing, but that she should be holy and without blemish. (Eph. 5:26)

Every husband is to be the spiritual leader and, in essence, the priest of his home. To fulfill this role, he must be obedient to God. Through his own obedience, his love for his wife will be pure, leading her to holiness. As the head of the home, the husband is not to condemn, show inconsistencies, or keep a record of faults and mistakes. His sanctifying love will draw her away from her faults and bring her out of the world's defilement, making her holier and helping her grow spiritually.

Husband, does your marriage have goals? Spiritual goals? Are you able to say that since you married your wife, she has become more devoted to God? The late Peter Marshall observed:

> We are souls living in bodies. Therefore when we really fall in love, it isn't just physical attraction. If it is just that, it won't last. Ideally, it's also spiritual attraction. God has opened our eyes and let us see into someone's soul. We have fallen in love with the inner person, the person who is going to live forever. That's why God is the greatest asset to romance. He thought it up in the first place. Include Him in every part of your marriage, and He will lift it above the level of the mundane to something rare and beautiful and lasting.

That puts it in perspective, doesn't it? True love is love with a purpose, and that purpose is to help your partner grow deeper spiritual roots.

4. Adoring Love: Love That Shows...and Tells

Finally, we see that husbands should love their wives with adoring, affectionate love:

So husbands ought to love their own wives as their own bodies; he who loves his wife loves himself. For no one ever hated his own flesh, but nourishes and cherishes it, just as the Lord does the church. (Eph. 5:28)

Our culture is preoccupied with bodies. The body is the means of advertising everything from cars to milk. Our culture's view of the body is out of balance, but Christians should particularly honor their bodies as they are the temples of the Holy Spirit. When the body is nourished and fit, the result is a sense of well-being. In the same manner, when a man loves his wife as his own body, she is nourished and loved affectionately, resulting in a sense of well-being, wholeness, and health. This adoring, physical love is an extension of the love the husband has for his own body, and the love Christ has for the church.

In order for the wife to experience this kind of love, the husband needs to demonstrate and *verbalize* it. Traditionally, and especially in certain cultures, sensitivity is not taught to men. Expressiveness and sensitivity are often viewed as feminine characteristics and, therefore, men are discouraged from developing them. As a result, men sometimes resist giving their wives the reassurance they crave. A husband might justify this behavior by saying, "She knows I love her; I told her so when we got married!" Jesus, however, demonstrated and *verbalized* His love. He told His disciples He loved them, and He showed His affection for them. When Jesus washed the feet of the disciples, He didn't do it because they were deserving and wonderful. He washed their feet to show His love for them. In spite of all their weaknesses and negative characteristics, He made a decision to love them and demonstrate that love.

When a wife experiences her husband's unconditional, sacrificial love, she feels secure and finds it easier to submit. Without this security, she may fear that her husband will reject her for fickle reasons such as not liking what she's wearing or because she has gained a pound or two. This conditional love can result in a self-protective wife who resists submission. The cycle perpetuates as the husband grows angry and tries to grab the authority.

Husbands, remember when you were dating your wife, and you thought she was completely awesome and wonderful? Recall the feelings you had for her on the day you proposed. On your wedding day, you were overflowing with feelings of love as you watched her walk down the aisle. You treated her like a queen, opened doors, sent flowers, told her you loved her so much you would do anything for her. Think for a moment about the way you treat her today.

Unfortunately, we often find that our behavior has changed dramatically. Now, when she wants you to open the car door, do you growl, "What's the matter, got a broken arm?" I'm not speaking about every man, but there is a tendency and temptation to neglect the romantic, adoring kind of love we had for our wives in the beginning. We should remember that little things mean a lot, such as sending flowers, being kind, showing affection, and going out of our way to treat her like a queen. We need to do that again.

Yes—But

One of the biggest obstacles to experiencing the blessings of the God-intended roles of marriage is our tendency to play the "Yes—But" game. It goes like this, "Yes, I know I'm supposed to love my wife as Christ loved the church, but I can't love her that way until she submits to me." Or the wife might say, "Yes, I know I should submit to my husband, but he doesn't cherish me like a Christian husband should." This is a double-bind situation that sets up conditions that can stall and endanger a marriage.

Instead, change your focus from *getting* what you want, to *giving* what your spouse needs. This is all part of submission to the Lord. The Bible calls it "dying to self"—a concept which couldn't be more at odds with the worldly view of self-esteem. Yet as the following explanation shows, dying to self results in a Christlike life and fulfilling relationships:

Dying to Self

When you feel forgotten, neglected, and sting with insult or oversight, you can still be happy—you have been counted worthy to suffer for Christ. That is dying to self.

When your good is evil spoken of, when your wishes are crossed, your advice disregarded, your opinions are ridiculed, and you refuse to let anger rise in your heart or even defend yourself, but you take it in patient, loving silence, that is dying to self.

When you lovingly and patiently bear any disorder, irregularity, or annoyance; when you can stand face to face with waste, folly, extravagance, spiritual insensibility, and endure it as Jesus endured it, that is dying to self.

When you are content with any food, any offering, any raiment, any climate, any society, any attitude, any interruption by the will of God, that is dying to self.

When you never care to refer to yourself in conversation or record your own good works; when you can truly love to be unknown, that is dying to self.

When you see your brother prosper and have needs met and can honestly rejoice with him in spirit and feel no envy or question God when your own needs are far greater and in desperate circumstances, that is dying to self.

When you can receive correction and reproof from someone of less stature than yourself, can humbly submit inwardly as well as outwardly, finding no rebellion or resentment rising up within your heart, that is dying to self.

What on Earth (or in Heaven) Should We Do?

Without divine guidance, we can become accommodating in the wrong ways. Rather than changing our life-style to conform with the Word of God, we tend to change our theology to conform to the way we live. People end their marriages and justify their actions with statements like, "I believe it was God's will."

Let's affirm what the Scripture says and decide to live it by God's grace. We won't find peace and fulfillment in our marriages until we are determined to be committed to performing our God-created roles.

All the marriage books and seminars on earth will only be a temporary bandage for our wounds. We must submit to Jesus Christ and be controlled by the Spirit of God. For some that may mean making the first-time decision to surrender your life to Jesus Christ and become a Christian. For all of us, it means we must stop *looking* for the right person and strive to *be* the right person.

Remember, God's design for marriage wasn't haphazard or faulty. If we are submitted to the Lord and to each other in our marriages, we will experience what God intended—a marriage that is a little glimpse of heaven right here on earth.

Sam Levinson once said, "Love at first sight is nothing special. It's when two people have been looking at each other for years that it becomes a miracle." Make those marriage knots secure by tying them right in the first place!

Chapter Six

Uneven Strands:
When a Christian Is Married
to an Unbeliever

Variety, as the saying goes, is the spice of life. Millions of couples have experienced the truth of that maxim in their own marriages. For instance, he likes the covers off at night; she's cold in a goose-down sleeping bag. He wants the toilet paper to roll over; she wants it to roll under. He's a morning person; she stays busy until after midnight.

We're all different, and that's part of the joy as well as the challenge. While our differences mean we must adjust, they can also bring couples closer together. Whether in a physics class or a relationship, opposites still attract. A man will readily admit being attracted to a woman because she is so different from himself.

There are some differences, however, that are so fundamental and profound that they could threaten the long-term stability of the relationship. Scripture draws special attention to the situation of the *unequally-yoked* marriage—in other words, a believer married to an unbeliever. This situation can bring dramatic stresses to the ties of marriage.

What on Earth Is an *Unequal Yoke*?

Perhaps you've heard Christians refer to an "unequally-yoked" relationship. You may have pictured everything from an uncooked egg to an unevenly sewn article of clothing. In reality, Paul borrowed this ancient farming term to illustrate how people fit together:

> *Do not be unequally yoked together with unbelievers. For what fellowship has righteousness with lawlessness? And what communion has light with darkness? And what accord has Christ with Belial? Or what part has a believer with an unbeliever? And what agreement has the temple of God with idols? For you are the temple of the living God. (2 Cor. 6:14-16)*

When Scripture was written, people lived closer to the land and were familiar with farming techniques and agriculture. When planting a crop, farmers used oxen to plow the fields. A yoke was a harness-like wooden bar that linked two animals with U-shaped pieces which fit around their necks. It was designed to hold the animals' heads in place and keep them moving at the same pace and in the same direction as they pulled their loads of equal weight. As long as the two were work animals of the same size, weight, and strength, the yoke was painless.

Picture now an ox yoked to a pony. As the ox moves deliberately and forcefully forward, the pony bucks and lurches, trying to race off in another direction. The yoke binds, pinches, and weighs heavily on their necks while their painful journey drags on.

Picture once more the yoke. Now imagine a Christian who loves the Lord, seeks His will, hungers for the company of other believers, and has a heart yielded and softened to God, yoked in marriage to a unbelieving spouse who is baffled by these yearnings. Paul's graphic image becomes heartbreakingly accurate.

The Scripture *strongly* warns Christians not to be unequally yoked together with unbelievers. In doing so, we are mismated in the same way righteousness is mismated with lawlessness and light is mismated with darkness. Yet many people find themselves in exactly this situation with all the problems that go with it. Here is one wife's description of her situation:

> I am saved, my husband is not. We are separated because I am saved. Divorce—is it a sin? When I talk to the Lord about it I am so dull of hearing, I can't hear what He has to say.

In those few painful lines, her confusion and disillusionment are evident. She yearns for God's voice.

Sometimes, this situation can arise from a marriage which appeared to be between two believers. Perhaps one has backslidden or may have deceived his spouse by pretending to be a Christian:

> How do I, as a woman, deal with a spouse who is not interested in God, Christianity, or church anymore?

This is a hard question born out of the frustration of trying to pull the marriage plow in different directions.

So, what can we do if we find ourselves in an unequally-yoked marriage? While the answers are not always easy, God has not left us without hope.

How Does Being Unequally Yoked Happen?

There are several circumstances which result in un equally-yoked marriages. Each has unique problems and challenges. While both husbands and wives can find themselves in the situation of being married to an unbeliever, for the sake of simplicity, and because it is *most* often the case, the husband will be referred to as the unbeliever (no ill-will intended) in these illustrations.

One Heard His Voice

Here is a common scenario: Two unbelievers fall in love and marry. After the marriage, the wife may sense her need to get right with God. When she does, her salvation instantly results in an unequally yoked marriage. She was not disobedient. On the contrary, she was *very* obedient. She did not sin. She simply responded to the Lord drawing her to Himself. She made the smartest decision she could ever make.

But oddly, this wonderful choice can be a threatening development in a marriage which had previously been between two unbelievers. Now that one person is a Christian, a marriage which had been stable may have hard times on the horizon. The believer faces the challenge of trying to influence her mate to Christ without alienating him. It can be a long, difficult process which may or may not result in a saved spouse.

One Fell Away

As in the above letter, the unequal yoke may be the result of two believers marrying and one of them deciding to go the way of the world. In the words of the writer, her spouse is "...not interested in God, Christianity, or church anymore." Suddenly, he wants nothing to do with matters of faith. He is backslidden and has left his spouse holding the spiritual bag. The believer may be especially hurt and grieving over the lost relationship she had with her spouse. Life at home may become frayed and tenuous. In this case, both partners are aware of the new status of their marriage: they are now unequally yoked. "For better or for worse" takes on a whole new meaning.

One Was Deceived

This is another painful scenario. At the time the couple married, she may have believed that her spouse-to-be was a Christian. Perhaps when they were dating, he said and did all the right things to convince her he was. He may have gone with her to church and Bible study and figured out how to speak fluent "Christianese." He may have purposefully deceived her because he wanted her to marry him, or he may have deceived even himself, believing he was a Christian because he went to church, was a moral person, and didn't belong to an obviously non-Christian religion.

One Is Reaping What Was Sown

When a Christian believer willfully dates and marries an unbeliever, that person is reaping what she has sown. She may have been attracted to his personality, his looks, or his good character. Perhaps she hoped that later she could influence him to become a Christian. Mistakenly, she tried to blend light with the darkness, with no more success than joining holiness with sin. When couples make up the marriage rules, they shouldn't be surprised by the outcome of spiritual incompatibility. Seeds of disobedience will yield a harvest of consequences.

Now, the couple is married and must work through the ramifications of those choices. Not a day will go by that she is not reminded of her disobedience to God and the consequences of her sin.

The Snares of Spiritual Singleness

The unequally yoked believer is caught between two dimensions: the worldly life with her husband and the spiritual life she holds in her heart and with other believers.

To her husband's bewilderment, the kinship she feels for other Christians sometimes surpasses her feelings of closeness with her own family. She privately grieves when she can't confidently turn to her husband for comfort and counseling; she mourns that her husband is not interested in spiritual matters. She bears the burden of their children's spiritual upbringing and worries about the effect of an unsaved father on their lives. Being spiritually single, she will be alone at some of the most important times in her life. She realizes that the spiritual issues she once minimized are the most important. Antoine de Saint Exupéry was right when he said:

> Love does not consist in gazing at each other but in looking outward together in the same direction.

Out of this conflicted situation come some unique problems and snares which pose dangers to the marriage.

Spiritual Vulnerability

When a Christian is deprived of the joy and stability of having a saved spouse, a special vulnerability can result, as we see in the following story:

> Connie was a wife who faced this pressure, and as often happens, someone saw her dilemma and responded. It began simply enough because they were both always alone at church functions. He would often fill that vacant, fourth chair at the table, and so they became good friends. Then they began sharing their problems of being alone in a non-Christian world. A cup of coffee, lunch, automatically sitting together in church, soon became their normal relationship. Their hands touched as they shared a hymnal and a spark of emotion grew into a small flame.
>
> It wasn't long before Connie began to wonder if maybe she should leave her husband and marry a Christian. It seemed that all of her problems would

then be solved. Life would be a blissful bubble of praying together, attending church together, reading the Scriptures together—absolute perfection.

With perfection as her goal, Connie began picking apart her own marriage. Small differences with her husband became large barriers. They quarreled often, and she determined more than ever to attain that blissful bubble of a Christian husband.

Satan knows our weaknesses. Like a woodpecker, he pecks until he finds our most vulnerable spot and then hammers us relentlessly. He can cleverly disguise sin as an appealing, even holy, alternative.

The Thoughtlessness of Others

I wish I could say that Christians were the most understanding and caring of all people. They should be, but that is not always the case. Well-meaning people within the Body of Christ can heap guilt and confusion on the spiritually single person. Sometimes their remarks are glib and thoughtless such as, "Unless you're married to a Christian, you're not really married in God's eyes." Baloney! To God, marriage is marriage. Marriage creates a one-flesh union, which is why we are cautioned so strongly to marry our own spiritual kind. Another common statement is, "Your marriage is really no different from a Christian marriage." Again, baloney! If there was no difference between an unequally-yoked marriage and a Christian marriage, the Bible wouldn't warn us about it so strongly.

Unequally-yoked believers hear more than their share of simplistic advice. People imply subtly and, often not so subtly, that if they were just doing the right thing, their mate would be saved. Comments range from, "Just be sweeter and more loving to your husband, and he will want to be saved," to "When God is finished with you, He will start working on your husband." And then there's the ultimate statement of the obvious, "Just pray about it." If only these folks knew the countless prayers that had been lifted up for the unbelieving spouse. Sometimes people have prayed for years and years with no sign of change or interest from their mate. These comments can heap a devastating amount of guilt on a believer.

The truth is, the only one responsible for the unsaved spouse's spiritual condition is the unsaved spouse. He is responsible for his own choice before God. No one can choose salvation for him, not even his believing mate. While God sometimes uses the influence of the spouse to draw the unbeliever to Himself, the believer is not responsible for the salvation of his or her spouse.

I came across a story about Charlotte Huddelston, who died at Fort McLellens Noble Army Hospital in May of 1983. She had breathed argon gas which had mistakenly been pumped into the oxygen system. The mix-up apparently occurred because the tall white tank of odorless, non-toxic argon resembled the tanks containing oxygen. Although argon alone wouldn't have poisoned her, it displaced the oxygen in her blood and resulted in suffocation. Thoughtless words can do the same thing by producing a weight of suffocating guilt that can smother spiritual vitality.

Overlooking the Good

Sometimes the problems that go along with having an unsaved spouse can dominate the believer's attention and overshadow many good things in the relationship. There may be a tendency to idealize Christian marriages, imagining that if the spouse was saved there would be no more arguments, disagreements, or wet towels left on the bathroom floor! We all know that the most committed Christian couple can experience upheaval in their relationship. By the same token, an unequally-yoked couple can share deep and wonderful experiences.

While there are extra pressures and pain, unequally-yoked marriages can still be good marriages. Obviously, unless both the husband and wife are serving the Lord, there will be many missed blessings, but the marriage itself can be loving and fulfilling. As James Dobson said, "The key to a healthy marriage is to keep your eyes wide open before you wed and half-closed thereafter."

When you look at a piece of white paper with a black dot on it, what do you notice? The dot! Even with so much white area around it, the dot captures our attention. When the greatest desire of a Christian man or woman is to have a believing spouse, the tendency may be to focus on this to the exclusion of the many good things in the relationship. To avoid driving your spouse away, focus on common interests and appreciate your marriage. As you do, pray and trust God to do His work in the heart of your unsaved spouse. Solomon wrote, "The discretion of a man makes him slow to anger, and his glory is to overlook a transgression."

The Blame Game

We Blame Ourselves

It's human nature to want to blame someone when we are having problems. However, believers tend to take the blame for their spouse's unsaved condition. As we discussed earlier, thoughtless comments from others can encourage that tendency. But apart from those influences, the believer is prone to worry that her shortcomings as a Christian have had a direct impact on her spouse: "If I was more loving, he would see Christ in me and want to become a Christian." Or, "Maybe if I was more submissive, or a better wife, he would be a Christian by now."

A believer who knowingly and deliberately marries an unbeliever is experiencing consequences which directly result from that sin. But each person makes his or her choice, for which God will hold him or her responsible. A husband or wife won't be able to stand before the Lord on Judgment Day and say, "Lord, it's not my fault, it's the mate You gave me." It didn't work for Adam in the Garden, and it won't work on Judgment Day.

We Blame God

After years of praying and claiming Scripture, a woman's husband is still not saved. She's tried to be the model wife: when he grumps, she's sweet; when he makes a last-minute excuse for not going to church, she smiles and says, "It's okay, honey," and goes alone. After a while, her patience wears thin, and she begins to get angry—with God. "Why is this so difficult, God?" she prays. "Are You too busy? Why can't I have a saved husband and a Christian marriage?" She feels like God doesn't care and has passed her by.

As much as she wants her spouse saved, keep in mind that God wants him saved even more. Remember that He "so loved the world" that He sent His own Son to die for him. God doesn't overlook anyone:

> *The Lord is not slack [or slow] concerning His promise, as some count slackness, but is longsuffering [patient] toward us, not willing that any should perish but that all should come to repentance. (2 Pet. 3:9)*

These words need to burrow deep into troubled hearts. It's not God's fault, and it's not the believer's fault either.

Who Is to Blame?

In a word—Satan. The blame should be placed upon the thief who has come to steal, kill, and destroy. Jesus said that Satan comes and snatches the Word that has been sown on the topsoil of the heart. When someone hears the Word of God and doesn't understand it, the wicked one comes and snatches it away. The natural man doesn't understand the things of the Spirit because Satan has blinded the minds of those who do not believe.

Don't misunderstand. We certainly play a part in people coming to Christ. Our lives can either repel or attract people to Him. Ultimately, however, the battle is waged between the lover of our souls and the enemy of our souls. The devil has vowed to hate anything God loves and to try to thwart His purposes for our lives by influencing our choices.

Years ago, C.S. Lewis penned his famous book, *The Screwtape Letters*, a fictional story based on real-life experience. In the book, a senior devil was training his nephew, Wormwood, saying, "I, the devil, will always see to it that there are bad people. Your job, my dear Wormwood, is to provide me with the people who do not care."

When you see an attitude of indifference in your spouse, remember there is something more going on than appears on the surface. An enemy is at work behind the scenes.

What can we do for our mates who are blind to spiritual matters? First, pray. Pray that the Holy Spirit will pry open that person's eyes so God's light can enter his mind and heart. Second, search the Scripture for down-to-earth guidance and encouragement so your marriage will be the best it can be.

Peter's Principles for Partnership

The complex issue of the "unequal yoke" is not unique to twentieth-century, occidental culture. It's been around awhile. Almost twenty centuries ago, the Apostle Peter discussed general principles for successful marriages; he even gave specific instructions to the wives of unbelievers. From the very beginning, Christianity produced domestic problems.

It may seem strange that Peter's advice to wives was six times longer than advice given to husbands. This was because the wife's position was far more difficult than a husband's. Wives had fewer rights in ancient times and, in some cases, were considered the *property* of their husbands.

If a wife converted to Christianity while her husband remained loyal to the ancestral gods, marital fireworks followed. Peter advised these women to be the best wives they could be under those tough conditions. He encouraged them by telling them their husbands could be won to Christ. William Barclay referred to this as "The silent preaching of a lovely wife":

> *Wives, likewise, be submissive to your own husbands, that even if some do not obey the word, they, without a word, may be won by the conduct of their wives, when they observe your chaste conduct accompanied by fear. Do not let your adornment be merely outward—arranging the hair, wearing gold, or putting on fine apparel—rather let it be the hidden person of the heart, with the incorruptible beauty of a gentle and quiet spirit, which is very precious in the sight of God. For in this manner, in former times, the holy women who trusted in God also adorned themselves, being submissive to their own husbands, as Sarah obeyed Abraham, calling him lord, whose daughters you are if you do good and are not afraid with any terror. Husbands, likewise, dwell with them with understanding, giving honor to the wife, as to the weaker vessel, and as being heirs together of the grace of life, that your prayers may not be hindered. (1 Pet. 3:1-7)*

Let's fly low and slow over this textual terrain to get a good look at exactly what he is saying.

Submission with Wisdom

In the preceding verses, the really tough word for wives to accept is "submissive." A wife who is unequally yoked reads that she should submit and feels she is in a double bind. How can she submit to an unsaved husband who is doing off-the-wall things and, at the same time, be submissive to the Lord and Christian principles? And woe to the wife with an unsaved husband who doesn't know any other Bible verse but the verse which tells women to submit! He will quote it and use it as a weapon against his wife.

Submission does not mean that the relationship between husband and wife is one of dictator/doormat. Peter was not referring to spineless submission but "voluntary selflessness." Submission means relinquishing your rights in favor of meeting the needs of someone else. It is the obedient response of a believer to the will of God. I heard about a woman who was married to a man she did not love. He was a demanding man who insisted she wait on him hand and foot, getting up every morning at dawn to cook and serve his breakfast. He was so demanding that, in trying to satisfy him, her life was miserable. Eventually, he died, and she remarried a man she truly loved. One day, she came across the list of rules her former husband had compiled. As she read through them, she was struck by the realization that she was fulfilling most of those requirements for her new husband. Now, however, there was a difference: she no longer acted out of fear or duty—but love.

There have been some wrong teachings by people who believe that no matter what a husband does, the wife should submit to him. Another teaching tells believing wives that if they trust God, He won't allow the unsaved husband to do anything outside of God's will. Ridiculous! Why assume that the husband no longer has free will now that his wife is saved? Beware of this kind of over-simplified advice. James Dobson shared the following letter from a wife whose relationship was ruined by following this philosophy:

Paul began to get interested in a beautiful divorcee who worked as his bookkeeper. At first, it seemed innocent, and he helped her in various ways.

I began to notice our relationship was deteriorating. He always wanted this other woman along whenever we went anywhere, and he spent more and more time at her house. He said that they were doing accounting work, but I didn't believe it.

I began to nag and complain, but it just made him more determined to be with her. Gradually, they fell in love, and I didn't know what to do about it. About this time, I bought a book in which the author promised that if I submitted to my sinner-husband, God would not allow any wrong to happen. I thought I might lose him forever, so I agreed to let the other woman come into our bedroom with us. I thought it would make Paul love me more, but it just made him fall deeper in love with her. Now, he's confused and doesn't know which one of us he wants. He doesn't want to lose me, and he says he still loves me and our three kids, but he can't give her up either. I love Paul so dearly. I begged him to turn our problem over to the Lord. I love the other woman, too, and I also know she is hurting. But she doesn't believe God will punish this sin. I have experienced terrible jealousy and pain, but I always put the needs of my husband and his lady-friend above my own. What do I do now? Please help me. I am on the bottom looking up.

There comes a time to say no— "No, I won't get drunk with you"; "No, I won't break the law with you"; "No, I won't live a sinful life-style with you." Submission to your husband does not mean submission to sin. First and foremost, be submitted to God. If submission to your husband conflicts with God's holy Word, *that's* the time to say no. As Peter put it, "We ought to obey God rather than men" (Acts 5:29). A believer married to an unbeliever must prayerfully balance submission with wisdom.

Wordless, Winning Ways

Peter's marital guidance was not lofty, ivory-tower stuff; it was practical, rubber-meets-the-road theology. He told us the actions we must take for marriage to work and zeroed in on the conduct of the believer married to an unsaved spouse. Again, while the example used here deals with a saved wife and an unsaved husband, these principles are the same for a saved husband and an unsaved wife.

In verse 1 of chapter 3, Peter said "...that even if some do not obey the word, they, without a word, may be won by the conduct of their wives." Peter cautioned believers against spiritual nagging. Even well-meaning efforts can impede the Lord's progress in reaching the unsaved spouse's heart. If his wife is constantly preaching to him, a husband can feel like the God Squad is after him! It is a natural human tendency to pull away when being pushed.

While nagging doesn't help, there are times when the believing spouse should talk about the Lord. When asked, she should be prepared to answer without preaching. Talking about spiritual matters too much will only result in her mate tuning her out and looking for a different frequency. However, if she talks about it rarely—and with sensitivity and discretion—he is more likely to listen.

Spiritual words and concepts are usually lost on unbelievers because they are neither interested nor keyed in to spiritual lingo. Our actions, however, communicate. Peter knew this when, in verse 2, he said husbands are influenced by their wives "...when they observe your chaste conduct accompanied by fear."

Observe is a key word which means "to notice and pay careful, close attention." The unsaved mate observes his wife's conduct and sees how she lives out her Christianity. More than words, sermons, or nudges, behavior is the most effective witness of faith. The believer's chaste conduct accompanied with *fear*, which means "appreciation" or "reverence," is being watched, absorbed, and weighed by the unbeliever on a daily basis.

The Holy Spirit must be given lots of elbow room to work in the life of an unbeliever. Without the obstacle of a pushing spouse, the unbeliever is able to see the issues clearly and make his decision before the Lord. He can't be forced—resist the temptation to slip Christian pamphlets in his tuna fish sandwich, pin notes to his pillow, or set the alarm to a Christian radio station. This only cheapens the gospel. Trust the Lord and get out of the way. Freedom to decide happens in the absence of manipulation.

Beauty: Balancing the Outward with the Inner

Who doesn't appreciate beauty? People have been drawn to beauty ever since Adam and Eve. In almost every civilized culture there has been a desire to beautify the body. That's okay. After all, if the barn needs painting, paint it! But looks should never be the mainstay of a relationship. Today, beauty product marketing represents an industry of almost seventeen billion dollars annually in the United States, with each individual spending about seventy dollars per year. Though there's nothing wrong with looking good, any relationship built solely on physical appearance is doomed to failure. After all, fighting age and gravity is a losing battle. That's why the writer of Proverbs 31 cautioned: "Charm is deceitful and beauty is passing, but a woman who fears the Lord, she shall be praised" (Prov. 31:30).

We men applaud you for wanting to look great but center your attention on cultivating the gifts of the spirit rather than concentrating only on outward beauty:

Do not let your adornment be merely outward—arranging the hair, wearing gold, or putting on fine apparel—rather let it be the hidden person of the heart, with the incorruptible beauty of a gentle and quiet spirit, which is very precious in the sight of God. (1 Pet. 3:3-4)

A survey of five thousand children revealed that, when choosing between four desirable characteristics, 48 percent said they wanted to be smart; 25 percent wanted to grow up to be beautiful; 20 percent admitted they would rather be wealthy; and only 7 percent thought it important to be wise. I wonder how much better we adults would fare? Don't you think it's time to grow up? Rather than wallowing in kid stuff, let's live our lives in pursuit of wisdom and eternal values.

Being attractive, taking care of yourself, and dressing nicely are fine things to do and are appreciated by most husbands. But Peter cut to the core issue when he told wives to let "the hidden person of the heart, with the incorruptible ornament of a gentle and quiet spirit" be the focus of her attention. Why? Because these are the qualities that set the believer apart from the world. Outward beauty will fade, but a gentle and quiet spirit is "incorruptible." In fact, these qualities grow more beautiful through the years. An unbelieving spouse may be full of doubt and confusion about many spiritual things but, in his own wife, he will witness the ageless beauty of a Christ-filled life.

Pay Attention!

As already mentioned, unequally yoked wives are torn between two worlds. They hunger for involvement with other believers and with the church. They want to be in fellowship, encouraged, and spiritually fed. That's fine and healthy, but the rub comes when these activities take them away from their spouse, causing feelings of loss and resentment. Peter used the past as a lesson for the present on this subject:

For in this manner, in former times, the holy women who trusted in God also adorned themselves, being submissive to their own husbands, as Sarah obeyed Abraham, calling him lord, whose daughters you are if you do good and are not afraid with any terror. (1 Pet. 3:5-6)

The word *obey* means "to pay close attention or attend to the needs of another." When we come to Christ, our priorities change. God is number one in our lives. When a wife (or husband) comes to the Lord, the spouse is suddenly bumped out of first place and the priorities can begin to look like this:

1. God
2. Church
3. Children
4. Spouse.

This change does not go unnoticed by the unbeliever, whose feelings may be hurt. His resentment is justifiable; after all, he hasn't changed—his wife has! Just because the husband is not a believer does not mean his needs can be ignored. The following letter illustrates an unbeliever's pain and confusion when his wife became a believer:

You have to remember what it's like when a man marries his wife. She's more than his lover, she's his whole life—his first priority. He never wants anything to come between the two of them. A man can have trouble accepting his own children because each new child takes so much of his wife's attention away from him. Suddenly, her main concern is for the children rather than for him. The only way he can tolerate their intrusion into his marriage relationship is that he also comes to know and love his children. But when a man's wife becomes a Christian, it's a whole different kind of threat. Suddenly, she has a love relationship with someone he can't even see. He can't understand anything she tries to tell him about this new God that she's come to know. All he knows is that she is in love with somebody else, and he's jealous. Instead of remaining the first priority in her life, as when they first got married, he has suddenly been demoted to number two after God. This is the way it must be for a Christian, but an unbelieving husband can't understand that at all. It would be easier for him to understand if she had run off with another man. But she's in love with someone he can't even compete with. He feels helpless. To make matters worse, she starts pressuring him to love her God, too. That really makes him resentful. It's worse than if, after they got married, his mother-in-law moved in, and she and his wife took sides against him. When she finds that she is unable to share her greatest joy with her husband, the wife starts craving fellowship. She can't wait to be with her Christian friends. She suddenly loses interest in her old friends because they're not Christians. So now the man and wife don't even have friends in common anymore. The husband feels that he hasn't changed—she has. She has broken the marriage contract. In his eyes, she is being unfaithful.

A husband needs the attention of his wife and to be esteemed and respected. If her relationship with the Lord places him at the bottom of her list, how can he help but resent Christianity? The structure for the marriage relationship has not changed because the wife has become a Christian—the husband is still the head of the home and deserves the attention and respect of his wife.

Mutual Respect

Respect is a fundamental human need. As children, our parents' respect is every bit as vital as their love if we are to feel we have value in the world. Lacking this, we can spend our lives seeking some form of affirmation or power.

In pagan cultures before and during New Testament times, there was no respect in the marriage relationship. Demosthenes accepted it as the rule of the day: "We have courtesans for the sake of pleasure; we have concubines for the sake of daily cohabitation; we have wives for the purpose of having legitimate children and being faithful guardians of all the household affairs." Xenophon, the Greek historian, claimed that husbands wanted a wife whom they "might see as little as possible, hear as little as possible, and ask as little as possible." Socrates in a similar vein queried, "Is there anyone to whom you entrust more serious matters than to your wife, and is there anyone to whom you talk less?"

Respect is also vital to the well-being of marriage. When husbands and wives respect each other, they are lifted to higher capabilities and possibilities. Scripture emphasizes the mutuality of respect and esteem:

> *This is a great mystery, but I speak concerning Christ and the church. Nevertheless let each one of you in particular so love his own wife as himself, and let the wife see that she respects (or honors) her husband. (Eph. 5:32-33)*

Respect is not a one-way street. Peter specifically told us that the husband is to honor his wife:

> *Husbands, likewise, dwell with them with understanding, giving honor to the wife, as to the weaker vessel, and as being heirs together of the grace of life, that your prayers may not be hindered. (1 Pet. 3:7)*

Honor means "to assign worth" and is manifested verbally and practically. We can start by telling our spouse, "Honey, you're precious to me, I love you and respect you." Then follow it up with actions. By listening to one another and valuing the opinions and ideas of our mate, we are demonstrating our love. Respectful behavior never undermines or corrects our spouse in front of others.

Fight Fire with Showers of Blessings

Peter gave some very practical instruction for successful relationships. He first reminded us to be "of one mind, having compassion for one another...." Wives, remember when you decided to marry your spouse? You spent countless hours planning and setting goals together. Has that stopped? You should *still* be beside your mate, wholeheartedly involved in your marriage and future. Your position as a believer in Christ does not mean your position as a helper and companion at your husband's side has changed.

Same for you, men. If your wife is still an unbeliever, let your lifestyle draw and convince her. In all the everyday matters, be compassionate, tenderhearted, and courteous toward her. In most marriages these refinements tend to fade with familiarity. Don't let your marriage follow suit. Think of the respect and courtesy we show our friends. Should we show less to our own spouse?

Finally, Peter reminded us not to sink to the level of "returning evil for evil." On the contrary, when a wrong is done to us, we should return blessings. Revenge may temporarily satisfy our ego, but it can spell doom to a marriage, particularly between a believer and an unbeliever. Resorting to this childish attitude undermines the most fundamental principles of grace and forgiveness. In returning blessings to our mate in the midst of conflict, we are able to demonstrate Christ's love.

Time for a Motive Check

After all that has been said, can we guarantee that if you study, pray, and practice Peter's principles for partnership, your spouse will become a Christian? No, not necessarily. Naturally, that's our hope and God's desire, but remember, each person has a free will. Your prayers, words, and lifestyle will be an influence, but it's still your mate's choice.

As a believing husband or wife, our motivation for godly behavior should be *obedience*. Jesus told us to love, respect, and submit to our spouse—whether or not he/she is saved. Any other motive is an ulterior motive.

Regardless of the reason you are in an unequally yoked marriage, rest assured that you could not possibly want your spouse to come to the Lord more than He does. Whether God sovereignly placed you in the marriage relationship to influence your spouse and children, or whether you are there as a result of disobedience, you can depend upon God's grace. He desires that you have abundant life, being secure in the knowledge that He loves you perfectly. Remember, in your struggle you should be "casting all your care upon Him, for He cares for you" (1 Pet. 5:7).

Whether your mate will be saved today or fifty years from today, only God knows. In the meantime, bring your attention to building your marriage into a glorious reflection of Christ's love and grace.

Chapter Seven

When the Cord Comes Unraveled:
A Perspective on Divorce

Unravelling the Facts from the Fallacies

Flying home from the Middle East recently, I was talking with a woman on the plane about the issues of divorce and remarriage. Before long, something interesting began to happen—people seated around us began listening and joining the discussion. We had stumbled upon a gold mine of popular concern. In churches, too, divorce and remarriage are issues of great interest, concern, and controversy.

These are unpleasant issues because they are frequently subjects of debate and disagreement. There is no shortage of written material, both secular and Christian, on this painfully prevalent subject. Why, then, am I writing more? Divorce and remarriage are among the subjects questioned most often by Christians but least often addressed by the church. When I think of the children who are casualties in the war of ravaged relationships, I realize married couples need a good dose of biblical truth.

The Gallup Organization conducted a poll in which they questioned teens from divorced homes. They learned that 71 percent felt their parents didn't try hard enough to save their marriage. With that in mind, I want to cut through the maze of simplistic answers and philosophical fluff and raise the flag of truth on God's standard.

A Fresh View of Divorce

Approaches to the Bible

What is truth and where does it come from? Jesus told His followers to "Take heed how you hear" (Luke 8:18). Yes, there is even a danger that those who listen to the truth of Scripture can hear it differently than was intended. We tend to listen selectively, picking and choosing Scripture as though it was a celestial smorgasbord, holding on to that which allows us to maintain our comfort zone.

All of us have opinions on the subjects of divorce and remarriage, and I'm certain if we brought together twenty Bible scholars, they would have a diversity of opinions as well. However, as we approach this complex study of divorce and remarriage, we should be aware that our opinions can hinder us from hearing the truth.

We can either approach the Bible with a fixed framework of beliefs and arrogantly try to cram texts of proof into that framework, or we can humbly let the truth of Scripture provide the framework and build upon it in obedience to God's Word, with the cooperation of the Holy Spirit. Though it may not be possible to achieve total objectivity, the right attitude goes a long way.

The most faithful and fruitful way to approach the Scriptures is nakedly, with open hearts. As we embark on this study of divorce and remarriage, we should strive to approach these subjects without presupposition and be ready to have the truth unfold before us.

Like It or Not, Divorce Is a Fact for Christians

Divorce is a sensitive and difficult subject which is made more complex because it is saturated with feelings and emotions. Most of us have been touched in some way by divorce. Maybe our parents divorced when we were young; we may have friends or relatives who are struggling through the trauma of a dissolving marriage; or the issue may be much closer to home. Whatever the case, while confronting the issues, we must be sensitive to people suffering from divorce.

Many of the letters pastors receive deal with questions about marriage, divorce, and remarriage. People want to know if it is ever biblical to divorce and remarry and, if so, under what circumstances. One woman described her tangled situation:

> I am a divorced mother. I am dating a man who I must constantly remind that I will not have premarital sex. He tells me that if we got married now, it would be adultery anyway because I am still married in God's eyes. My ex-husband is married now, and I have become a Christian. Can I ever get married again?

The confusion surrounding divorce can challenge our fundamental need and right to spiritual security. Another portion of a letter reflects a genuine desire to know God's will for this divorcée's future:

> According to the Scripture, how does God feel about divorce, especially when there seems to be no other alternative? Then, if we ever remarry, are we adulterers? God's Word says that those who commit adultery will not enter His kingdom. Is this from divorce and remarriage? It says if we are saved we will not lose our salvation. I am confused. I am a born-again Christian going through a divorce, which I do not want, but it's inevitable. I am young, and I am sure I will remarry someday, but I don't want to commit adultery and not enter the kingdom of heaven.

These questions deserve answers. The Bible is a beacon of light shining through the fog of uncertainty and directing the wayward to safety. Providing direction for our lives is what God does best! If you genuinely want to know what God requires, the Bible is the Book for you. If you will take it to heart, the fog will dramatically lift. "But the path of the just is like the shining sun, that shines ever brighter unto the perfect day" (Prov. 4:18).

Although we sometimes struggle to understand what the Bible says about divorce, God's word on the subject is clear. Confusion is the result of sin entering the picture and clouding God's intent for relationships, marriage, and divorce. I am so thankful for this Book, written by God. It provides the wisdom and guidance to make relationships work and make them work well. God wants our relationships to be fulfilling, and they will be if we cooperate with Him.

The State of the Union on Marriage and Divorce

Ironically, while the river of marriage manuals and seminars rises steadily each year, our cultural standards for marriage, divorce, and remarriage are falling each year. Worldly guidance on these subjects doesn't go much deeper than personal opinion. The statistics and manifestations in our society are staggering. Consider some of these findings:

- The US Census Bureau provided the following figures: In 1920, there was one divorce for every seven marriages; in 1940 it rose to one out of every six marriages. In 1960 the ratio was one out of every four and, in 1972, one out of every three marriages ended in divorce. In the last century, the divorce rate has risen 700 percent. It is estimated that out of every 1.8 marriages, there is one divorce. If this continues, experts predict there will be more divorces than marriages resulting in an upside-down ratio which could bring about the demise of the family unit as we know it.

- Sweden has passed a one-day divorce law. If there are no children under age sixteen in the household, a divorce can be granted immediately, no questions asked.
- In Nevada, one judge handles so many divorces he does them in groups of fifteen couples at a time. He brags that he can sometimes grant as many as fifteen divorces in ten minutes.
- In California there is a best-selling book titled *How To Do Your Own Divorce*. It provides forms and instructions for getting divorced without hiring a lawyer.
- A British physician wrote a book titled *The Death of the Family,* in which he states, "The best thing human society could do is to abolish the family altogether."
- Kay Millet, a famous women's liberation advocate, wrote in her book, *Sexual Politics,* "The family unit must go because it's the family that has oppressed and enslaved women for so long."

This is the tide we're swimming against, folks. But, at the same time, society's "theme of the hour" is the importance of family. It may be support in name only, but I think people are awakening to the realization that God knew what He was doing when He invented the family unit.

Christianity Today published an article by Dr. Armond Nicholi, director of the Harvard Medical School, in which he affirmed the vital role of the family in any culture:

> If there is any one factor influencing the character development and emotional stability of an individual, it is the quality of the relationship that he or she experiences as a child with both parents. Conversely, if people suffering from severe non-organic or physical-related emotional illness have one experience in common—it is the absence of a parent through death, divorce, or some other cause. A parent's

inaccessibility physically and/or emotionally can profoundly influence a child's emotional health.

A quality relationship with the parents is vital to the foundational stability of a child. The common denominator for emotional illness is a damaged relationship with mom and dad. Nicholi goes on to list six trends he sees in America that are destructive to the family:

1. Mothers of young children working outside the home. Child rearing is being delegated to professionals who, in spite of training and good intentions, lack the vital ingredient that makes a healthy, stable child: love.

2. Frequent family moves. Fifty percent of the American population lived at a different address five years ago. This mobility trend prevents a sense of roots, belonging and, of course, long-lasting relationships.

3. The invasion of television. It is estimated that the next generation will spend one-fifth of their lifetime watching television. Therefore, an eighty-year-old person will have watched four thousand solid days of television.

4. The lack of moral control in society. Society doesn't present or promote absolute moral standards. Without moral guidelines, confusion, guilt, and immorality result.

5. Lack of communication within the home. One survey reported that the average father spends thirty-seven seconds a day with his child in one-on-one, meaningful contact.

6. Finally, the major cause of emotional problems and the major detriment to the family is, by far, divorce. He concludes:

> The trend toward quick and easy divorce and the ever-increasing divorce rate subjects more and more children to physically and emotionally absent parents. If this trend does not reverse, the quality of family life will continue to deteriorate, producing a society

with a higher incident of mental illness than ever before. Ninety-five percent of the hospital beds will be taken up by mentally ill people. The illness will be characterized primarily by a lack of self-control.

Dr. Nicholi estimates that there are thirteen million children under the age of eighteen with one or both parents missing from the household. He contends that this family breakdown is detrimental to children, spouses, and society as a whole. I agree, and so do kids.

People magazine ran an article a few years back about two children of divorce, Ryan and Lindsey Berdan, ages nine and seven. On Wednesday nights their dad takes them to the local mall for dinner and all the video games they can play. Ryan has a hot dog and cream soda; Lindsey orders pizza. After dinner they head for the video arcade where they play Skee Ball. But even in the artificial paradise of the mall, Ryan is quick to concede that he and Lindsey really want the family they don't have. Each week, while out with their dad, the kids quietly make a stop at the mall's wishing well. "We always throw a penny in," Lindsey says; "we wish that Mom and Dad would get back together."

Views on Divorce: The Historical Perspective

The Greeks: Three Strikes and You're Out

In order to understand how divorce applies in our lives today, we need to have an overview of the early attitudes toward marriage and divorce. Greek men, at the time of Christ, can be described in one word—chauvinists. Women had no rights, and wives were secluded and forbidden to go out in public alone. On the other hand, men were expected to have extramarital affairs. Such relationships brought no discredit or stigma; they were simply part of ordinary life. You may remember from previous chapters that Demosthenes laid down the accepted rules of practice: Every man should have a mistress for companionship, a concubine for sexual pleasure, and a wife to bear his legitimate children and be a keeper of the home.

In their society, marriage meant that men had permission to seek pleasure anywhere, while women were expected to be faithfully devoted to their husbands.

Men further justified their promiscuity by cloaking their behavior in worship. There were "sacred prostitutes" who catered to the desires of these immoral men. William Barclay tells us that the Temple of Aphrodite at Corinth had a thousand priestesses who were considered sacred courtesans. Their nightly stroll down the streets of Corinth gave rise to the proverb, "Not every man can afford a journey to Corinth." Many of these temples were built and maintained from revenues generated by prostitution.

Apparently, there was no formal legal divorce in Greece. A man could simply dismiss his wife in the presence of two witnesses. A woman, however, could not dismiss her husband under any circumstances. The only stipulation for a husband divorcing his wife was that he return her dowry intact.

The Romans: Marriage the Second or Twenty-Second Time Around

For the first five hundred years of Roman history, there was not one single recorded divorce. Ironically, when the Romans conquered the Greeks, Greek immorality began infiltrating the Roman world. So, it could be said that the Greeks also conquered the Romans—by corruption.

Divorce and remarriage were rampant. According to divorce records that were found, some women had as many as twenty-eight husbands. Juvenal, a Roman satirical poet, cited the case of a woman who had eight husbands in five years. Marcus Valerius Martialis tells of another woman who had ten husbands. It was a practical solution, therefore, to identify a particular year by the name of their husband at the time. Can you imagine their diaries—"Back in the year of Horace...."; "Then, in the time of Bruce." In view of the revolving husbands and wives, it's almost understandable that Roman men said: "Marriage brings only two happy days—the day when the husband first clasps his wife to his breast, and the day when he lays her in the tomb."

The Jews: Not A Simple Certificate of Divorce

With this backdrop of the Greek and Roman views of marriage and divorce, we can imagine how confused people were on this subject by the time Jesus came along. While there was a great deal of confusion about divorce, the Jews viewed marriage as sacred. It was seen as a holy duty that all men were bound to undertake. If a man refused to marry and have children, the Jews felt he had broken God's command to "be fruitful and multiply." In fact, they believed marriage was so holy and vital that unmarried men were included on their list of seven categories of people who would not enter heaven.

As a result, marriages were sometimes prearranged when the couple was very young. Often the groom-to-be and bride-to-be didn't meet each other until they were engaged! Sometimes these young people were unhappy and resentful because they had been bound to someone they found undesirable or with whom they were incompatible. Out of these negative circumstances arose the ideology of permissive divorce. Therefore, Jesus' emphasis on infidelity as the only grounds for divorce struck a particularly sensitive nerve with the Jews:

"Furthermore it has been said, 'Whoever divorces his

wife, let him give her a certificate of divorce.' But I say to you that whoever divorces his wife for any reason except sexual immorality causes her to commit adultery; and whoever marries a woman who is divorced commits adultery." (Matt. 5:31-32)

This was tough stuff for these guys to hear. Many of them chose to rely on the teachings of the rabbis who saw things their way. "A woman," said the Rabbinical law, "may be divorced with or without her will, but a man can be divorced only with his will."

The rabbis were very familiar with the Old Testament passage Jesus referred to from Deuteronomy regarding the certificate of divorce:

"When a man takes a wife and marries her, and it happens that she finds no favor in his eyes because he has found some uncleanness in her, and he writes her a certificate of divorce, puts it in her hand, and sends her out of his house, when she has departed from his house, and goes and becomes another man's wife, if the latter husband detests her and writes her a certificate of divorce, puts it in her hand, and sends her out of his house, or if the latter husband dies who took her to be his wife, then her former husband who divorced her must not take her back to be his wife after she has been defiled; for that is an abomination before the Lord, and you shall not bring sin on the land which the Lord your God is giving you as an inheritance." (Deut. 24:1-4)

The Jews knew this was what the Scripture said, yet they held a variety of opinions regarding the meaning Moses had in mind. The "million shekel" question was, "What exactly did Moses mean when he referred to uncleanness?"

Two schools of thought eventually dominated. Rabbi

Shammai, a "thinker," believed that uncleanness referred only to sexual immorality. To him, adultery was the only permissible cause for divorce. Rabbi Hillel, a liberal, interpreted the word in the widest possible sense. He said uncleanness referred to anything a husband didn't like about his wife. This included such offenses as not preparing his dinner the way he liked, letting her hair down in public, or being a brawling woman who could be heard at the neighbor's house. According to his permissive interpretation, Rabbi Hillel felt all these were legitimate grounds for divorce. It should come as no surprise that his was the most popular interpretation among the men.

As a result, men divorced their wives for any and every reason—it was the ultimate no-fault divorce for husbands. To the rabbis, the most important issue was that the letter of the law had been followed, culminating in a "certificate of divorce" at the termination of the marriage.

By the time of the New Testament, divorce had become so easy that the institution of marriage was on the endangered species list. Many girls were refusing to marry because marriage lacked security and a sacred foundation. That was the status quo of the times. Then—enter Jesus. Jesus rocked the theological boat with the truth.

Jesus' View: Remember the Master's Plan
What God Has Joined Together: The Ultimate Super Glue

When Jesus asserted that the only allowable reason for divorce was sexual immorality, He caused tremendous upheaval and emotional fireworks. The Pharisees let a little time pass, but they were just waiting to test Him further on the subject:

> Now it came to pass, when Jesus had finished these sayings, that He departed from Galilee and came to the region of Judea beyond the Jordan. And great

multitudes followed Him, and He healed them there. The Pharisees also came to Him, testing Him, and saying to Him, "Is it lawful for a man to divorce his wife for just any reason?" (Matt. 19:1-3)

Notice how carefully they phrased their inquiry? The question revealed their strongly-held beliefs about divorce. Jesus, rather than arguing the text with them or dwelling on their misconceptions, took them back to the very beginning—the Master's plan for marriage:

And He answered and said to them, "Have you not read that He who made them at the beginning 'made them male and female,' and said, 'For this reason a man shall leave his father and mother and be joined to his wife, and the two shall become one flesh'? So then, they are no longer two but one flesh. Therefore what God has joined together, let not man separate." (Matt. 19:4-6)

Jesus set the record straight by essentially saying, "Look it up! God invented marriage. It was His idea to bring a man and woman together. Don't mess with God's invention!" They needed to hear that God esteems the marriage relationship which He invented and empowered.

To understand how God feels about divorce, we must first understand how He feels about the union of marriage. Jesus plainly struck a blow to their traditional views by saying, "...but from beginning it was not so." It is vital that we grasp this: divorce was never part of the Master's plan for marriage. If it had been part of the plan, we would have to believe that God created the one-flesh union of marriage knowing it might one day end in an amputation of the relationship by divorce.

Have you ever played with super glue? It's amazing

stuff. But if you make the mistake of getting it on your fingers and allowing them to touch for a couple of seconds, they will be sealed together as though they were "one flesh." The only way to separate them is to forcefully pull them apart—taking a layer of skin as you do. There is no easy way to divide one flesh.

The Bible says that in marriage, the husband and wife are similarly glued together, and God views them as one flesh. To divorce because of a problem in the marriage is an extreme and inappropriate solution, much like cutting off a hand because there is a splinter in a finger.

Divorce: The Result of Hard Hearts

Pharisees weren't the kind of men to back down, and this was one battle they didn't want to lose. They insisted on arguing their case with Jesus by quoting (actually, misquoting) the Old Testament Scripture regarding the certificate of divorce. Jesus responded by taking them back to the Book, long before the Deuteronomy Scripture had been written, to the very beginning when God made man and marriage:

> They said to Him, "Why then did Moses command to give a certificate of divorce, and to put her away?" He said to them "Moses, because of the hardness of your hearts, permitted you to divorce your wives, but from the beginning it was not so. And I say to you, whoever divorces his wife, except for sexual immorality, and marries another, commits adultery; and whoever marries her who is divorced commits adultery." (Matt. 19:7-9)

Notice their misconception. The Pharisees asked Jesus why Moses had "commanded to give a certificate of divorce." Where in the entire Old Testament did Moses command that a divorce be given? Divorce was a concession, not a commandment. Jesus pointed out that it was because of people's hard hearts that this concession was granted. Marriage was divinely planned and instituted; divorce, in contrast, was instituted by man. God regulates divorce and, in some cases, He permits it, but it was not part of His plan for marriage. One pastor likened this compromise of divorce to a man who designed and installed a beautiful swimming pool. The man envisioned long, cool, leisurely swims in crystal-clear water on hot summer days. To his disappointment, the crystal water became tainted with germs, causing the water to be invaded by slimy, green algae. The more water he put in, the greener it became. This certainly was not in his original design. So he had to choose; either he could fill up the hole and abandon his beautiful design for a swimming pool, or he could add chlorine and other chemicals that would change that green, murky water back to pretty, crystalline water. A concession had been made for dealing with the bad, in order to preserve what was good.

Similarly, in allowing divorce in some cases, Moses made a concession in order to preserve the plan of marriage. Like all concessions, divorce comes at a great cost. The question is—can you afford it?

Contemporary Perspectives on Divorce

Things haven't changed all that much from ancient times. There were scads of opinions about both marriage and divorce, and there still are. If you've been around Christian institutions, you have discovered there are countless opinions and theories about divorce for Christians. At one extreme are those who believe divorce is never allowed by God under any circumstances, and at the other extreme are those who say divorce is not a big deal. The Bible doesn't agree with either of these views.

Accommodating Theology

Unfortunately, we live in an age where people are separating for every conceivable reason and then trying to find a Scripture to justify their actions. This "accommodating theology" is like a Christian form of "situational ethics." Trying to find a verse to justify divorce compromises Christian marriages and causes them to succumb to the same failure rate as non-Christian marriages. Instead of making vows for "as long as we both shall live," the promises are being subtly changed to mean "as long as we both shall love." Many decide in advance that marriage will last only as long as they feel in love with each other. When a spouse's beauty begins to fade, hard times come along, or they enter a low cycle in the course of their growth as a couple, they conveniently forget that a vow is a promise. When that happens, it's easy to believe that one has the contractual right to divorce.

Even Our Leaders Let Us Down

Divorce is rampant even among Christian leaders. Some are divorcing their wives, going out with their secretaries or women from their congregations, and still maintaining their leadership and pulpit positions. On a recent tour of Israel, our guide told me of an American Christian leader who went on one of his tours and told him that Jesus had appeared to the leader saying he could let his wife go because He had somebody better for him. Hello! Is anybody home?

A pastor of a church in New York managed to retain his pastorate in spite of an attempt to oust him. After admitting he had an affair with a married woman in the congregation, the pastor divorced his wife of twenty years. He made it clear that he was planning to marry the woman with whom he had the affair. There were some who wanted to fire the pastor, asserting that he violated the ministerial code of sexual ethics. But the errant minister had supporters who said he'd done nothing wrong since the woman was a willing partner, and the relationship was not exploitative.

The Apostle Paul warned Christians not to be "...conformed to this world..." (Rom. 12:2). The result of these myriad views is the threatened disintegration of the family unit.

Shortly before his death, the Duke of Burgundy was presiding over the Cabinet Council of France. A proposal was made by the ministers that would have violated a treaty but secured important advantages for the country. Many good reasons were offered to justify the deed. The Duke listened in silence, and when all had spoken, he placed his hand upon a copy of the original agreement, and said firmly, "Gentlemen, we have a treaty!" He was a leader who valued his promises.

Godly Marriages Mean Fewer Divorces

We should be alarmed about the effects of divorce on society, children, the family unit, and the family of God. But, as Christians, our primary concern should be that divorce violates the principles for marriage set forth by God. If there is any hope for saving marriages, it will be found by going back to personal devotion to God and the obedient study of God's Word.

I believe the church has a tendency to ignore and downplay divorce because the problem is so widespread even among Christians. In order to avoid upsetting people, accommodation becomes the trend.

To counteract the problem of divorce, church leaders must begin by being discriminating about performing weddings. If the church comes alongside couples and helps them lay a solid, relational foundation, they will provide the necessary "ounce of prevention" that can help secure marriages. Let's slow down a bit and be determined to do it right! The combination of premarital counseling and making sure that both people are committed believers will prevent the tragedy of an unequal yoke. Some couples resent this rigorous process, but for those who want their marriages to have staying power, they will welcome the time of preparation.

God's View of Divorce—He (Still) Hates It. But...

Viewing the historical and contemporary perspectives on divorce is one thing, but the most important question we can ask is, "What does God think about divorce?" In the midst of accommodating theologies and worldly opinion that marriage and family are archaic institutions, God's opinion has never wavered. He was never more blatant on the subject than when the prophet Malachi preached:

> ...Because the Lord has been witness between you and the wife of your youth, with whom you have dealt treacherously; yet she is your companion and your wife by covenant. But did He not make them one, having a remnant of the Spirit? And why one? He seeks godly offspring. Therefore take heed to your spirit, and let none deal treacherously with the wife of his youth. "For the Lord God of Israel says that He hates divorce, for it covers one's garment with violence," says the Lord of hosts. "Therefore take heed to your spirit that you do not deal treacherously." (Mal. 2:14-16)

Why would God be so adamant about this human failure and sin and use such strong language to convey His feelings? Because He loves us and wants to spare us the heartache and destruction brought about by divorce. Though many view divorce as an escape, God knows that often the guilt and loneliness people experience are more tragic than living with their problem.

Don't misunderstand. While it's true that God hates divorce, God loves the divorced person. The church must come to grips with this and extend God's love to the divorced. We will gain more perspective on this sensitive issue in the next chapters, but remember, let your focus be restoration rather than reproach. Walk softly around a broken heart.

Doris Mae Golberg, from Rochester, Minnesota, wrote about the loss and loneliness she experienced when she became divorced:

> I have lost my husband, but I am not supposed to
>   mourn.
> I have lost my children; they don't know to whom
>   they belong.
> I have lost my relatives; they do not approve.
> I have lost my friends; they don't know how to act.
> I feel I have lost my church; do they think I have
>   sinned too much?
> I am afraid of the future,
> I am ashamed of the past,
> I am confused about the present.
> I am so alone,
> I feel so lost.
> God, please stay by me,
> You are all I have left.

Chapter Eight

To call me a judge is something of a misnomer. I am really a sort of public mortician. In the past eleven years I have presided over the funerals of twenty-two thousand dead marriages. The trouble is this: I have buried a lot of live corpses. There was no sure way to discover and resuscitate the spark of life that surely remained in many of them.

—A Judge of the Court of Common Pleas, Toledo, Ohio

From Seamless Garment to Tattered Shreds: Divorce and the Christian

Paradise Lost

Reality has a nasty way of shattering the fragile veneer of our fantasies, doesn't it? "Real life" elbows in and, suddenly, our expectations are shot down in flames.

We sit in our living rooms and passively buy into the illusions created by TV commercials. We go to the restaurant that advertises the tempting-looking dishes, but the food staring up at us from the plate doesn't even remotely resemble those pictures. We watch the car commercial that shows a beautiful woman smiling contentedly as she glides down the highway in her new convertible. But when we buy the same car, we find ourselves sweltering in traffic with a payment book at home that will take us well into the next century.

Unfortunately, we often bring the same unrealistic expectations into our relationships. The bride who believed she'd married a handsome knight in shining armor discovers he has an irrational preference for wearing a smelly old sweatshirt when he's at home. The man who expected his wife to be a perpetual fairy princess wonders just when she turned into a frog!

149

How do we Christians reconcile "real life" with our faulty expectations? Is there something or someone to blame—fairy tales—our spouse—God?

God has a plan for each and every marriage. When our expectations collide with reality, it often seems that divorce is the answer. But when a couple decides to call it quits, they have actually chosen to reject God's plan for their marriage.

A Matter of Perspective

Some have argued that God's Word on divorce is inconsistent and, therefore, cannot be confidently followed. They concede that Jesus spoke against divorce twice in the book of Matthew, but since He didn't repeat it in Mark, Luke, and John it doesn't count. Why not? How many times does God need to repeat Himself before we count it as truth? Was Jesus only kidding in Matthew's gospel but serious in the other three? Should some of Jesus' words be changed from red ink to black? This is illogical and ridiculous. God did not address every facet of marriage and divorce every time these subjects were mentioned. A comprehensive understanding of marriage and divorce comes by virtue of walking through the entire biblical landscape.

As a first step through this terrain, let's explore the intent of the four gospels. Why would the Bible contain four accounts of the same basic material? God chose these four venues with their unique emphasis, perspective, and intended audience as a means of revealing His Son to the world. Therefore, each gospel contributes to our full understanding of the Person and teachings of Jesus Christ.

In Matthew, Jesus was presented as the Messiah of Israel, while Mark saw Him as the ultimate Servant of His Father. In Luke, Jesus was portrayed to the Greeks as the Son of Man or the ultimate Man. Contrast this to John's gospel which showed Jesus as the Son of God, deity in human flesh. If one gospel doesn't contain something included in the others, that doesn't mean it's not true; it only means it was not central to the intention of the author who penned that book. Conversely, if one writer included something the others didn't, it only verifies that the four writers didn't copy each other's writings. Each writer faithfully recorded Jesus' life and teachings with their own special accent. Keep this in mind as you pour over what Jesus taught concerning divorce and the Christian.

Looking for Loopholes: Semantics and Divorce

I've learned something about human nature. When we want to justify something bad enough, the Bible is never good enough! Like a lawyer looking for loopholes, some people imagine truth to be as pliable as a rubber band. Believe it or not, some say that Jesus was not even referring to marriage when He spoke of divorce in the following verse:

> *"And I say to you, whoever divorces his wife, except for sexual immorality, and marries another, commits adultery; and whoever marries her who is divorced commits adultery." (Matt. 19:9)*

What did He have in mind here when He spoke of divorce? Some argue that Jesus was speaking of a broken *engagement* because at that time, the Jews had an unconsummated, binding betrothal period of one year. It has even been suggested that He was referring to a separation rather than a divorce. This is inconsistent with the situation and context of the verse.

Jesus referred to the one being divorced as a wife and described the initiator of the divorce as one who, after the divorce, "married another." That certainly indicates that he had been married to the first woman, doesn't it? Jesus was talking about a married couple who had forsaken the marriage bond.

Of additional significance is the Greek word Jesus used

here for divorce: *apoluo*. Most Greek scholars agree that *apoluo* refers to "the divorce of a consummated marriage"; a one-flesh union that has been broken off, as opposed to a broken engagement or betrothal. This is the same word He used in all gospel texts when referring to divorce.

The context of this passage in Matthew is a significant factor in understanding the meaning. When Jesus and the Pharisees were discussing divorce, they didn't have to stop and define or explain the term. Jesus didn't say, "Now, let Me tell you what I mean by 'divorce.'" In its obvious context, the Pharisees knew He was referring to marriage because they had come to ask Jesus questions regarding marriage. The subject didn't change until the discussion was finished.

When Jesus referred to the Genesis account of the first couple, He wasn't referring to an engagement, nor was God when He said, "For this reason a man shall leave his father and be joined unto his wife and the two shall become one flesh." Jesus quoted this passage to illustrate that from the beginning, divorce was not part of the Master's plan for marriage. His sole concern was where these leaders stood with regard to God's original intention and design for marriage. To assert that this passage refers to an engagement period is not sustained by the context, the Greek grammar, or the background.

My concern is that we tamper neither with God's Word nor His design. The Christian should not try to justify himself but should strive to glorify God. Once we detour from God's plan and travel the road of excuses, we will have a hard time getting off. Eventually, however, the regret that comes from disobeying God will catch up to us, as exemplified in this exchange from Ann Landers' column:

Dear Ann Landers:

Ten years ago I left my wife and four teenagers to marry my secretary with whom I'd been having an affair. I felt I couldn't live without her. When my wife found out about us she went to pieces. We were divorced. My wife went to work and did a good job educating the boys. I gave her the house and part of my retirement fund.

I am fairly happy in my second marriage, but I'm beginning to see things in a different light. It hit me when I was a guest at our eldest son's wedding. That's all I was—a guest. I am no longer considered part of the family. My first wife knew everyone present, and they showered her with affection.

She remarried, and her husband has been taken inside the circle that was once ours. They gave the rehearsal dinner, and sat next to my sons and their sweethearts.

I was proud to have a young pretty wife at my side. But it didn't make up for the pain when I realized that my children no longer love me. They treated me with courtesy, but there was no affection or real caring.

I miss my sons, especially around holiday time. I am going to try to build some bridges, but the prospects don't look very promising after being out of their lives for ten years. It is going to be difficult re-entering now that they have a stepdad they like.

I'm writing in the hope that others will consider the ramifications before they jump. Just sign me

—Second Thoughts in PA

Check out Ann's unsympathetic response:

Dear Second Thoughts:

I could use the rest of this column to reflect on "sowing and reaping," but it would serve no useful purpose. I'm sure you also know that a father can't disappear for ten years and expect his sons to welcome him back with open arms. Sorry, Mister, your wife has earned their respect and devotion, and what's left over is going to the man who is now making their mother happy.

I'd say for this man, the fantasy is over— "real life" has set in!

Sexual Immorality: A Study of a Few Greek Words

Sometimes we forget that God created sex. He not only planned it as a means of propagating the earth, He wanted it to be a source of pleasure for mankind. God intended sex to be enjoyed exclusively within marriage. Within marriage, sexual pleasure is enriching, but outside of marriage, it brings defilement and long-term devastation. This is not a puritanical opinion—it's pure truth—no ifs, ands, or buts!

What, exactly, does *sexual immorality* mean? The King James Version translates this word as "fornication," while the New King James Version translates it as "sexual immorality," and the New International Version calls it "marital unfaithfulness." Basically, they all mean that we are not to have sex with anyone or anything other than our spouse, or the bond of oneness will be undermined.

The Greek word Jesus used is *porneia,* from which we get the word pornography. Both words share the same root meaning of any illicit sexual intercourse. Don't buy into the deception that porneia refers only to sex before marriage and not illicit sex after marriage. The argument to defend that viewpoint contends that if the writer had been referring to adultery, he would have used the word *moichao*, the Greek word commonly used for adultery. Therefore, they reason, the reference must be to the betrothal period during which an engaged (officially unmarried) person violates the agreement by engaging in premarital sex. This is absolutely foreign to the text.

Scholars agree that *porneia* is a broad term that covers every single kind of illicit sexual immorality: homosexuality, child molestation, bestiality, prostitution, *and* adultery. *Moichao*, on the other hand, refers only to one kind of illicit sexual intercourse—sex outside of marriage.

By using *porneia*, the Bible refers to and condemns all forms of sexual immorality, so no one can focus on one area and say, for instance, "This was just a homosexual act—I didn't commit adultery." No doubt, Jesus chose the word because of its categorical meaning, and He wanted no misunderstanding when He specified that the only grounds for a divorce is sexual immorality. *Any* illicit sexual behavior would so undermine the oneness bond that, in such cases, the innocent one could dissolve the marriage by divorce.

With this concession, Jesus was not advocating divorce. Far from it! He simply acknowledged that there are times when divorce does not lead to sin or adultery. Jesus had already told the Pharisees in no uncertain terms that, unlike themselves, He did not tolerate divorce for simply any reason. If they divorced for any other reason except one, they would be guilty of adultery.

The Pharisees were religious folks who were experts at putting holiness on parade. They may have felt puffed up with pride, thinking that because they hadn't technically hopped in bed with another woman, they weren't guilty. But Jesus told them that every time they looked at a woman and inwardly lusted after her, they were adulterers. In Jesus, they found someone who exposed their hypocrisy because He held God's ideal dear to His own heart:

> *"You have heard that it was said to those of old, 'You shall not commit adultery.' But I say to you that whoever looks at a woman to lust for her has already committed adultery with her in his heart."* *(Matt. 5:27-28)*

Ouch! I'm sure a lot of men fidgeted nervously when He said that! Jesus showed that God's standard went beyond outward actions and concentrated on the motivations and intentions of the heart.

The thought-life is where sin begins; the evil thought gives rise to the evil deed. Every time those ancient religious leaders allowed a spouse to be put away for unlawful reasons, they proliferated adultery. Groundless, rampant divorce caused these men and women to be guilty of adultery.

The Divorce Concession

There were valid grounds for divorce—as in the case of a spouse involved in sexual immorality. Jesus' concession for divorce was far more confining than the Pharisees', but it was completely consistent with the standards set forth by Moses and God. He reinforced His Father's original marriage blueprint and reiterated the truth stated in Deuteronomy 24: "...defilement occurs in the form of adultery when there is divorce for any reason other than sexual immorality."

Like people today, the ancient Pharisees weren't satisfied with that. They sought to broaden the path of leniency and allow divorce for almost any reason. The result was a heap of twisted Bible texts and devastated relationships.

Ancient Jerusalem and modern America have more in common than we might think. In ancient Israel, it was common for a husband to impulsively dump his wife and head for greener pastures just as happens today. Nowhere is this more apparent than in Tampa, Florida, where there is such an emphasis on speedy, convenient divorces, they actually have drive-through divorces!

The Effects of an Unbiblical Divorce

Immeasurable pain lines the path of every divorce. Anyone who has been through the process knows something of the isolation, hurt, resentment, and frustration divorce brings. Children may be the most affected, with resulting problems that last well into adulthood.

A survey of 2,867 people conducted by the University of Michigan revealed that children of divorce are more likely to suffer from adult depression than children who lost a parent to death. The loss experience from divorce is profound. In the following letter to Ann Landers, a man looked back on his own life and the impact of the divorce he initiated:

> Eleven years ago, I walked out on a twelve-year marriage. My wife was a good person, but for a long time she was under a lot of stress. Instead of helping her, I began an affair with her best friend. This is what I gave up:
>
> 1. Seeing my daughter grow up.
> 2. The respect of many longtime friends.
> 3. The enjoyment of living as a family.
> 4. A wife who was loyal, appreciative, and who tried very hard to make me happy.
>
> Ann, tell your readers that anyone who is married and has his or her next mate all lined up is looking for trouble. People don't know what they are giving up until they no longer have it. Then it's too late.

Our Relationship to God Suffers

There is someone else who suffers greatly from every divorce—God. Our relationship to God is affected by divorce. Although He loves us and will always forgive us when we repent, the classic response of a person divorcing for selfish reasons is a distancing of him/herself from God. Many drop out of fellowship, steer clear of Christian friends, and forget where they put their Bibles. They know they're doing wrong, and therefore they lack confidence in approaching God. Others may seem unabashed and continue to do the "church thing," while in reality, they are galaxies away from God.

During the turbulent years of ancient Israel, many men divorced their wives and married pagan women. This was directly against God's ordinance. As if that wasn't bad enough, they kept coming to God in pious worship. God finally confronted them with their sin and duplicity:

> *And this is the second thing you do: You cover the altar of the Lord with tears, with weeping and crying; so He does not regard the offering anymore, nor receive it with goodwill from your hands. Yet you say, "For what reason?" Because the Lord has been witness between you and the wife of your youth, with whom you have dealt treacherously; yet she is your companion and your wife by covenant. (Mal. 2:13-14)*

Oh, they were still coming to the Temple piously weeping, but it was a superficial show. They would not admit any wrongdoing and, as a result, God turned a deaf ear to them, rejecting their worship and offering. God didn't accept their worship because they hadn't done right by their life-long partners—their wives. Significantly, this is the only time in the entire Old Testament when the word *companion* was used when referring to a wife. Often, in the Old Testament, it described the relationship between best friends like David and Jonathan. God intended the marriage relationship to be one in which the husband and wife are best friends who nourish each other through that friendship.

Josh McDowell believes that the "sexual revolution" experienced in our culture over the last fifteen years is really nothing more than a search for intimacy:

> Most of our young people do not want the physical aspect of sex, they want someone who cares. They want to be able to care. They want intimacy. We have allowed our culture to dictate to us that the only way you find intimacy is through the physical—and that's an absolute lie!

God confronted the people and told them their sin made their worship meaningless. By divorcing their wives, they had sinned against the very ones who should have been their best friends. Their veneer of pious behavior was a sin against the Lord, so they lost intimacy both with their mate and their Master!

This may sound harsh and burdensome. My intention isn't to make anyone feel bad. God invented marriage and, therefore, He has the right to state what He thinks about its termination. God hates divorce for all the reasons the victims of divorce do—and more. He hates what it does to the children. He hates how it ruins families. He hates the way it zaps our spiritual and emotional life. He hates the resulting proliferation of adultery. He hates how it separates us from Himself.

That's why He compared the effects of divorce to a soiled garment. The separating of those involved in the "one flesh" agreement of marriage can only be an ugly and violent process. The guilty are covered with sin as surely as a murderer's clothes are splattered with the blood of his victim.

This is what God thinks of divorce: He hates the sin that causes it and the violent result. It goes against His Word and renders worship meaningless in His sight.

But...God Understands Divorce!

God speaks strongly against divorce because, from personal experience, He understands the pain it brings. In an analogous sense, God was a divorced person. His people turned their backs on Him by worshipping at other altars. As a result of their disobedience, they broke the covenant of love and their spiritual relationship. God said to the children of Israel:

> *"Then I saw that for all the causes for which backsliding Israel had committed adultery, I had put her away and given her a certificate of divorce; yet her treacherous sister Judah did not fear, but went and played the harlot also." (Jer. 3:8)*

God divorced Israel and put her away for the adultery she had committed. Although He was clearly the "innocent party" in this divorce, He didn't simply walk away. God loved Israel regardless of her sin and desired to restore the relationship, for restoration is always in God's heart. He never acted frivolously because He knew the pain it caused all the way around. For those who have been through divorce, or are going through divorce, God understands your pain firsthand.

With Jesus Christ, forgiveness, redemption, and repair are available. Talk with God about His restoration plan for you. As you do, you'll realize that although your sin be as scarlet, He can make you whiter than snow. Failure is not the last word. God has not pledged to smile only on those who have never blown a marriage relationship. Have you failed? Have you sinned? Then you've come to the right

Person—Jesus. The meaning of His name says it all, "for He will save His people from their sins" (Matt. 1:21).

Finally, a few words to my Christian brethren who may think I haven't been heavy-handed enough. "C'mon, Skip!" they may be thinking, "don't give this a light touch; divorce is contributing to the moral decline of our nation!" Hey, I know divorce is sin, which is precisely why it can be *forgiven*.

Allan Emery, a co-laborer in the Billy Graham Evangelistic Association, tells of an experience which made a deep impression on him. One night his father got a call informing him that a well-known Christian was passed out on a sidewalk—drunk. Immediately, his father sent his chauffeured limousine to pick up the man. Meanwhile, his mother prepared the guest room. My friend watched as she turned down the beautiful coverlets, revealing the mono-grammed sheets on the exquisite, old four-poster bed.

"But, Mother," he protested, "he's drunk. He might even get sick."

"I know," his mother replied, "but this man has slipped and fallen. When he comes to, he will be so ashamed. He will need all the loving encouragement we can give him."

There's a time for confrontation and rebuke, but there's also a time for restoration and repair. Aren't we thankful God didn't write us off? Isn't it time we helped people live obediently by extending a hand of fellowship? A pat on the back is only a few inches way from a kick in the pants, but it's miles ahead in results!

Chapter Nine

Deep down in my heart I wish I could find a good man who loved the Lord and lived as the Lord commands. I really yearn for companionship, even if it is just friendship. I've been married three times and had to support them all.

—Excerpt from a letter

Patching Up and Moving On:
Remarriage

If we could travel in a time machine to ancient Corinth, we might not feel as out of place as we would imagine. Though removed by culture and time, we would see some amazing similarities. In fact, some of the Corinthians' actions would make Hollywood stories pale in comparison. The sinfulness in Corinth was so rampant it was legendary. The word *korinthiazesthai*, which meant "to live like a Corinthian," became part of the Greek language and was a byword for evil, drunken living and a life of debauchery.

Remarkably, in spite of the immoral climate, God did a great work in Corinth. Many people had come to faith in Christ in the midst of rampant homosexuality, promiscuity, bestiality, and prostitution. As the gospel penetrated that culture, lives were changed, and that meant changes in relationships as well.

As might be expected, the people in the church at Corinth were confused and had questions about how to conduct their lives now that they were Christians. They wrote to Paul asking specific questions about divorce and remarriage and how God's relational principles applied to:

- believers married to believers,
- unbelievers married to believers, and
- widows within the church.

Today, people still wrestle with these problems and questions. That's why the Bible is so contemporary. Human nature being what it is, each generation faces these issues afresh. The following letter not only shows the confusion about the Bible's teachings on these subjects, it reminds us of the pain, disappointment, and sadness that go along with divorce:

> Tomorrow I will be married for six years, but it's not a happy occasion because we are going through a divorce. I met my husband in a Bible study. We would study the Scripture together, pray together, go to Christian activities, but then we got married and things changed. If this divorce does go through, I probably will not marry again for the kids' sake and also to follow the Lord's way. But I'll be honest, deep down in my heart I wish I could find a good man who loved the Lord and lived as the Lord commands. I really yearn for companionship, even if it is just friendship. I've been married three times and had to support them all.

That letter could have been written by a person from any generation. The desire for godly companionship and relationships has prevailed throughout time. But what is this woman to do? She's been "up to bat" on three occasions and struck out each time. She's come to the point where she feels the game is over, and it's time to sit on the bench.

It's not a news-breaking fact that many marriages in our culture are "second-time-around" marriages. In fact, being married more than once is so common that about 25 percent of the weddings taking place in a given year are second or third marriages for both the bride and the groom, and almost fifty percent of marriages involve one person who has previously been married.

Before we can live in accordance with God's Word, we have to *know* God's Word. In this chapter we will explore what the Bible tells us about divorce and remarriage.

Danger: Rationalizing Thoughts Ahead!

When experiencing difficult times in our relationships, we humans are inclined to rationalize our thoughts and behavior. People often burst out of their stressful situations like magma from a volcano. In their pain, they tend to go with the flow and take the easiest escape route. Be careful! The wounds and lingering resentment of the past can cause vulnerability. It's easy to rationalize that just getting out of the situation is the best way to handle things. But is it really?

There are situations, however, in which the marriage has been so violated that biblical divorce and remarriage are permissible. The burning question is, what are those situations and circumstances? Like the queries of the Corinthians, this is one of the more frequently asked questions in the modern church. As we seek answers, again, be careful! Looking for a new relationship on the heels of a broken one can lead to more heartache. Don't allow today's hurt and bitterness to dictate future decisions.

Sorting It Out—Who Can Remarry?

Not many of us would envy the job of educating and guiding the believers in Corinth on the subjects of divorce and remarriage. He knew his words would be the only light cast on these subjects because of the dark moral climate. Some couples had been living together before their conversions. Others had multiple marriages and divorces. The situations were complex, and there were no easy, pat answers. Paul was faced with such challenging questions as, "If a person has become a Christian, should he divorce the unsaved spouse and marry a believer?" And, "If a married Christian couple divorces can they remarry other people?" By the inspiration of the Spirit of God, Paul methodically focused on each situation.

Four Circumstances for Biblical Remarriage

Taking the words of Paul and Jesus together, let's look at four situations in which remarriage is an option:

1 and 2: Remarriage for Widows and
Those Divorced Before Coming to Christ

Paul addressed those who were single due to the death of a spouse in the following verses:

> *But I say to the unmarried and to the widows: It is good for them if they remain even as I am; but if they cannot exercise self-control, let them marry. For it is better to marry than to burn with passion. (1Cor. 7:8-9)*

The word *widows* is pretty self-explanatory; these are people who were formerly married but are now separated from their spouse by death. These individuals are free to remarry, as are those individuals who have never married.

Paul himself was dedicated to singleness and the unhindered worship and service to the Lord it allowed, but he recognized that this could be a disastrous choice for some. Corinth, like our own society, tolerated immorality. In such an environment, it was particularly tough to resist temptation. Therefore, to the unmarried and widowed who were not similarly directed to singleness, Paul recommended marriage.

Who, then, are the *unmarried*? The Greek word *agamos* literally means "without a marriage." The same term in verses 10 and 11 refers to those people who were previously married and are now divorced. Paul seemed to be speaking of people who were divorced before coming into a relationship with Jesus Christ.

When a person marries and divorces before salvation, remarriage is certainly permissible. Unless we know God through His Son, Jesus Christ, we cannot know God's plan or His will for our lives. How could we understand God's requirements regarding the hallowed, lifetime commitment of marriage? Paul tells us in his letter to the Corinthians:

Therefore, if anyone is in Christ, he is a new creation; old things have passed away; behold, all things have become new. (2 Cor. 5:17)

That little word *new* is an important one. It means "fresh"— as in a fresh start! Jesus used it when He spoke to His disciples about a *new* Covenant based upon the shedding of His blood (Matt. 26:28). When anyone places his trust in Jesus Christ, he is like a brand-new, fresh creation. The reversal of God's order caused by sin has been set right. God washes the chalkboard of the heart clean; no smudges remain. When a person repents, God cleans every sin, including divorce. If not, that would mean that divorce is the only sin not covered by the blood of Jesus Christ. Let the powerful words penned by David sink into your heart:

For as the heavens are high above the earth, so great is His mercy toward those who fear Him; as far as the east is from the west, so far has He removed our transgressions from us. (Ps. 103:11-12)

Like a brand-new baby, the newly converted Christian has no past before God—only a future! That's *amazing* grace!

3. Remarriage for a Believer When an Unbelieving Spouse Leaves the Marriage

In 1 Corinthians 7, we find the situation of a Christian married to an unsaved spouse. This was not an uncommon problem for the Corinthians, many of whom became believers only to be confronted with the realization that they were married to pagans. Should they stay in the marriage or leave it and seek a Christian relationship? Should they seek to become and remain single?

Those were tough questions that needed suitable answers. Their initial reaction may have been to put away their unsaved spouse by divorce so they would not be "unequally yoked." But Paul put an immediate halt to this faulty thinking. In verse 12 he said, "But to the rest I, not the Lord say...." Remember, earlier in verse 10, Paul emphasized that he was repeating what Jesus had said in relation to believers divorcing. Now, in verse 12, he clarified that Jesus didn't talk about this specific circumstance, so this guidance came from himself as further revelation from God. Paul was not stating an opinion but simply acknowledging that God had not given previous instruction on this issue. He, through the Holy Spirit, would now fill in the gaps:

Now to the married I command, yet not I but the Lord: A wife is not to depart from her husband. But even if she does depart, let her remain unmarried or be reconciled to her husband. And a husband is not to divorce his wife. But to the rest I, not the Lord, say: If any brother has a wife who does not believe, and she is willing to live with him, let him not divorce her. And a woman who has a husband who does not believe, if he is willing to live with her, let her not divorce him. For the unbelieving husband is sanctified by the wife, and the unbelieving wife is sanctified by the husband; otherwise your children would be unclean, but now they are holy. But if the unbeliever departs, let him depart; a brother or a sister is not under bondage in such cases. But God has called us to peace. (1 Cor. 7:10-15)

In Corinth, the unsaved spouses were sometimes angry that suddenly their wives or husbands were no longer interested in drinking with them or going to the wife-swapping parties down at the Temple of Aphrodite. Instead, their believing spouses were now praying and wanting Christian fellowship. Some of these unbelieving spouses wanted out of the marriage. The Christian would, of course, have no control over such a situation. In this case, the Christian is not to insist or plead that the unbeliever stay if he or she is bent on leaving.

To clarify his directive not to divorce a spouse who was willing to live with the believer, in verse 14 Paul explained the benefits for the unbelieving spouse and family:

For the unbelieving husband is sanctified by the wife, and the unbelieving wife is sanctified by the husband; otherwise your children would be unclean, but now they are holy. (1 Cor. 7:14)

Sanctified does not mean the unbelieving spouse is saved, but he/she is set apart in a special way so that God can bless the believer and the children. It is a sanctification of the marriage rather than a spiritual sanctification. In God's view, the home is set apart to be blessed and influenced by God when one or more family members become believers. The unbeliever and the children have the great advantage of living with the potentially saving influence of the believer. I often hear how the gospel penetrated a home through the faithful witness of one person. One by one, the whole family may come to know Jesus Christ.

An illustration of sanctification can be found in the account of Sodom and Gomorrah. God was tired of the unrelenting sin of the people there and decided to destroy them. Abraham bargained with God, asking Him to spare the cities if he could find fifty righteous people living there. God agreed, but Abraham soon learned his goal was unrealistic and asked God if He would settle for forty-five righteous people—then forty—and finally ten. God agreed to spare the cities if Abraham could find just ten righteous people. He was willing to allow His blessings to pass on to many wicked people for the sake of a handful of His own. Abraham found those ten, and thousands of wicked people were spared by the preserving salt of the righteous few.

In this same way, the blessings of the believer are enjoyed by the unbelieving spouse and the entire household. The best thing a believer can do for an unsaved husband or wife is to stay in the home and be that influence. Think of the potential of a sanctified home! I agree with Barbara Bush who said:

> At the end of your life you will never regret not having passed one more test, not winning one more verdict, or not closing one more deal. But you will regret time that you did not spend with a husband, a friend, a child, or a parent. If you have children, they must come first. Our successes in this society depend not on what happens in the White House, but what happens inside your house.

Think of what could happen in your house if the gospel finds its way into the hearts of all your family members! That would be true success. Unfortunately, it doesn't always happen that way. Sometimes the unbeliever decides to ditch the relationship. If that's the case, Paul says to let them leave:

But if the unbeliever departs, let him depart; a brother or a sister is not under bondage in such cases. But God has called us to peace. (1 Cor. 7:15)

Although it may sound harsh, remember, Jesus said He did not come to bring peace but a sword. Christ knew that because of Him, there would be division in the family. He recognized that son would be set against father, daughter against mother, brother against sister, and husband against wife. Sometimes, this is what happens when one person comes to know the Lord.

While Paul said to let the unbelieving spouse depart, he did not mean to force that person out. He didn't advise, "Push that heathen spouse out of the house." Care must be taken *not* to drive away the unbelieving spouse claiming the *technical* grounds for divorce have been met. This passage refers to the permanent, voluntary departure on the part of the unbeliever. Then, the believing husband or wife "...is not under bondage in such cases. But God has called us to peace." The New Testament translated by James Moffet says, "He is not tied to the marriage bond any longer." Kenneth Weist, in his expansive Greek New Testament puts it, "A brother or a sister is free from the indissoluble union of marriage."

4. Remarriage as an Option
When Sexual Immorality Has Violated the Bond

We've already looked at Jesus' own words in Matthew 19 regarding divorce due to sexual immorality:

"And I say to you, whoever divorces his wife, except for sexual immorality, and marries another, commits

adultery; and whoever marries her who is divorced commits adultery." (Matt. 19:9)

Since we've previously examined this at length, let's touch on it solely in regard to remarriage. When a partner has violated the marital bond by a sexually immoral lifestyle, and he/she is no longer willing to remain as a faithful partner, the innocent party is free to divorce and remarry. However, in this scenario, divorce is only an option given because of human sin and failure; it is not an obligation.

But What if Both Husband and Wife Are Christians?

When Paul penned his Corinthian letter, he left no stone unturned regarding marriage and divorce. Anticipating this question, he spoke about the union between married believers:

Now to the married I command, yet not I but the Lord: A wife is not to depart from her husband. But even if she does depart, let her remain unmarried or be reconciled to her husband. And a husband is not to divorce his wife. (1 Cor. 7:10-11)

It isn't clear why some of the Corinthian believers wanted to divorce. Perhaps some thought they would be able to live holier lives more devoted to God if they were single. There were probably some who wanted a more desirable mate and cloaked it in a wish for a more spiritually fulfilling life.

Paul's phrasing was important when he said, "I command, yet not I but the Lord." He wanted to make it clear that he wasn't making this up as he went along but was repeating what Jesus had said in the gospels. If a Christian is married to another Christian, they should not separate, depart from one another, or divorce—they should stay married and work through their problems.

Today, couples in the church need to hear that. "'Til death do us part" wasn't added to the marriage ceremony just for kicks; the stability of home and country depend on it. Seventy-five percent of divorced people remarry, and sixty percent of them have children. If current trends continue, in a few years, stepfamilies could outnumber traditional families. Christians, it's time for us to work through our marital disagreements and show the world that God's idea of marriage can work for God's own children.

If, however, the husband and wife divorce, they have two options. If the divorce occurred for any reason other than sexual immorality (porneia), they are *not* free to remarry but can remain single the rest of their lives, or they can be reconciled to each other. This is not pop-psychology or marriage counselor advice; it is God's mandate.

If there has been sexual immorality by one of the partners, divorce is allowed as a divine concession to human sin. It is an option, permissible, but not commanded. Jesus does not encourage divorce; however, He understands sin and its effects. Divorce and a subsequent biblical remarriage is a provision for the preservation of the innocent party.

There Is Another Way

Even in marriages where a spouse has committed adultery, there can be reconciliation and forgiveness. The same God who gave Israel a divorce also said He would forgive backsliding Judah, and her sins and iniquities He would remember no more. I've seen forgiveness mend broken marriages and watched Christians, crushed by the weight of an unfaithful spouse, decide to keep the marriage together rather than pursue divorce.

I once worked with such a lady in California. She had an unbelieving husband who broke the marriage bond by sexual immorality. Not only did he have an adulterous affair, he had a child with the other woman as well. After this, he divorced his wife and walked out of the relationship, leaving behind the debris of shattered lives. His Christian wife could easily have chosen to date and marry another man. Her husband committed sexual immorality and, as an unbeliever, he departed from his wife. Technically, she was free on two counts, and she knew it! However, she felt no peace in her heart to pursue another relationship. Instead, she waited, hoped, and prayed. Some of her Christian friends told her it was hopeless and encouraged her to move on and find a Christian man. Four years later she was still waiting. Even her counselor felt it was time for her to move on. But she continued waiting and trusting God. Her prayers were finally answered. Her ex-husband genuinely repented and turned his life over to God. Where there once had been heartbreak and ruin, there was now reconciliation and forgiveness. Not long after that, I had the privilege of performing their second marriage ceremony—to each other!

I don't share this story as a formula, nor do I mean to imply that in every case the unbeliever will return and both parties will live happily ever after. I'm saying that God's power and ability to reconcile is far greater than most of us dare trust Him for. This woman's testimony stands out as a bright beacon of God's unending grace in a marriage.

Hosea Knew

In the Old Testament book of Hosea, God told Hosea that He wanted to use his life as an example of forgiveness and reconciliation to His people. Hosea was to marry a prostitute by the name of Gomer. It must have caused quite a stir in Israel, as the people gossiped about the prophet who married a harlot. Shame, shame, shame!

God knew this woman would run around on Hosea and have affairs and children by other men. But even while she was in the midst of sexual immorality with other men, God wanted Hosea to provide for her. Then, when she was wasted and ruined, God told Hosea to bring her back, reconcile the relationship, and forgive her. God made these stiff requirements for the prophet because He wanted this same reconciliation to happen between Himself and His people—the children of Israel:

> *O Israel, return to the Lord your God, for you have stumbled because of your iniquity; take words with you, and return to the Lord. Say to Him, "Take away all iniquity; receive us graciously, for we will offer the sacrifices of our lips...I will heal their backsliding, I will love them freely, for My anger has turned away from him. I will be like the dew to Israel; he shall grow like the lily, and lengthen his roots like Lebanon." (Hos. 14:1-2, 4-6)*

Scripture raises us to a higher ideal of love, forgiveness, and reconciliation. This is the heart of the gospel, just as the heart of God is forgiveness. I believe that reconciliation, when possible, is always God's highest ideal. Certainly Hosea would be the first to say it's not easy. But as difficult as it may have been for him, God provided the power to pull it off. He will give us the power, too.

But It's After the Fact—Now What?

We've covered a lot of territory in both the Old and New Testaments about marriage, divorce, and remarriage. After reading and praying, some may realize for the first time that they have been, or are presently, involved in a sinful relationship or an unbiblical divorce. They may be saying, "I've blown it in a big way. Oh, God, I've sinned. What do I do now?" Well, there is good news for these folks. At the heart of the gospel is the assurance that if we bring our sins before Jesus Christ, everything we have ever done in the past is brought under His blood and forgiven.

Thankfully, we live in the grace of forgiveness that David described in his writings (remember, David knew all about being forgiven for violating a marriage):

> *The Lord is merciful and gracious, slow to anger, and abounding in mercy. He will not always strive with us, nor will He keep His anger forever. He has not dealt with us according to our sins, nor punished us according to our iniquities. For as the heavens are high above the earth, so great is His mercy toward those who fear Him; as far as the east is from the west, so far has He removed our transgressions from us. (Ps. 103:8-12)*

Forgiveness, Yes, But Also a Higher Calling

Non-believers divorce for many reasons, and why would we expect otherwise? What should we expect sinners to do, if not sin? Apart from God they are capable of nothing else. For Christians, however, the ideal is God's Word, and when we live accordingly, our behavior will be different. Obedience to God should begin at the point of realization of failure, whether we've blown one marriage, two, or three. While God is anxious to forgive us, we must make a vital decision to lay hold of the truth and be obedient to Him. For you, obedience may mean a reconciliation with an estranged spouse, or halting the proceedings of an unbiblical divorce, or simply being obedient in your present marriage. Whatever truth applies to the situation, you must now be obedient to God's ideal. Determination to obey God will allow Him to raise us to His highest, wherever we are.

You can trust that God will bless you as you endeavor to do His will. In either case, the safest and best attitude before God is one of humble compliance. Your prayer should be,

"Lord, after learning what I have, I am determined, with Your help, to obey, because I love You above all."

If you are in the sad position of facing divorce, or if you are already divorced and considering remarriage, now is the time to come to the Lord openly, ready to receive His words of guidance. The obedience required may seem like an unbearable burden, but when you know God's will for your life and you are obedient, you will find peace and strength as a result. The following story shows how obedience can become the pathway that leads to freedom and joy:

> It was the summer holiday and a city boy went for the first time to a farm in the country. He found a lot of things to interest him. In particular, he always liked to watch the farm servants going to the well for water at the bottom of the field. They put on a kind of wooden yoke which fit onto their shoulders with two large buckets hooked on each end. The weight rested on the yoke and the servants had to steady the buckets with their hands.
>
> This boy, like a lot of others, found it very hard to obey. He was always happy when the holidays came because now he could be his own boss for awhile. But he found that even in the country where there was no home-work and no teachers, he still had to do what other people told him to do. That night, when he came back from the well, he wanted to stay up, but he was told that it was past his bedtime and he had to go upstairs. So he went, grumbling to himself, "Wait 'til I grow up. I'll be my own boss and nobody will tell me what to do."
>
> The next morning, to his surprise, he seemed to be back in the city again. As he dressed and put on his jacket, he was amazed to find that it had a wooden yoke on the shoulders which he could not remove. Just then, the maid walked in and she, too, had a yoke of wood

on her shoulders. When he went to breakfast, his mother had one, too. When Dad came downstairs, sure enough, he had the heaviest yoke of all. The world seemed very strange that morning. Before school, the boy sat down with a picture book that he was very fond of, but, somehow, the pictures looked different today. Everyone appeared to wear a yoke: soldiers, sailors, drivers, shoppers, policemen. At last, he came to a portrait of a king and queen and looked carefully at it. Even the king had a yoke on his shoulders. It was made of gold and adorned with diamonds and rubies. It looked very heavy. Then, suddenly, a thought struck. *I guess even grown-ups have to obey, too. Even kings and queens. That's why they have a yoke on their shoulders like the rest.*

The next picture that the boy looked at represented the Lord, standing with a multitude of sick people. On Jesus' shoulders there was also something. At first glance it looked like a heavy yoke, but it also looked like wings, folded up. Perplexed, the boy muttered to himself, "A yoke—wings? I don't get it." Slowly, a thought dawned on him. "I wonder if a yoke does not get to be like wings? I wonder if when we serve and obey we are happier and do our work more easily like the little birds?" Well, it was now time for school. As he walked down the street, looking at the people, he noticed another strange thing. There were some people who didn't have a yoke on their shoulders. "Aha!" he cried. "There are those who don't need to obey!" But, as he looked again, he saw that none of those people could move freely because they were dragging a very heavy weight after them, fastened to their ankles. It was much worse to bear than any yoke. They had escaped the yoke, but they were prisoners. At last, it became clear to him. "I see!" he cried. "People who will not obey and do not serve have a weight to drag because they are idle. Or they have chains to carry because they are so selfish." In his excitement, he turned to hurry home.

In a moment he awoke. It was only a dream. He was lying in the little farmhouse bedroom. There was no wooden yoke on his jacket, but he woke up a little wiser. He began to understand that even the greatest and bravest people had to obey so that they might serve others and serve God. They were both greater and nobler because they did obey.

As he prayed that morning, he said, "Oh, Lord Jesus, help me to be quick to obey and glad to serve and someday let my yoke be turned into wings, Amen."

Regardless of our station in life, if we are determined to obey God based on the information He has given to us in the Bible, we will be happier and more peaceful as a result. But the opposite also holds true: If we decide not to obey, thinking we have a better idea, we will be chained to our sin, and life will be much more difficult than if we simply bear the yoke of obedience.

Wanted: Compassionate Christians!

A word to those who have not been divorced and are in great marriages committed to God's ideal: I commend you for your standards and commitment. Your example is needed today more than ever. I applaud God's gracious hand in the molding of your relationships.

We must maintain biblical standards when dealing with divorced people while loving them with all we've got. Both are possible, you know. We must never sacrifice truth at the altar of love. Anyway, love based upon God is always truthful. Paul said we should be "...speaking the truth in love...." (Eph. 4:15).

People need the truth of God, but they need it mixed with tons of compassion and love. Kicking a sad and hurting person can only cause deeper wounds. He may have an even greater need for warmth and love because his experience has left him feeling isolated and unwanted, as expressed by a visitor to a foreign land:

> I lived for a number of years in a large city in a far-away country. The people seemed so different to me, and they knew I was different, too. Sometimes, I just walked the streets in the evening all by myself. I was very lonely. They all talked so funny. When they tried to talk to me, I would just nod my head as if I was agreeing with whatever they said and act as if I was in a hurry and had to leave. But every evening I would take my little walk. I lived there but never really felt like I belonged there. I was an outsider. Sometimes through an open curtain, I would see a family sitting around a table or snuggling around a fire in happy fellowship. Then the curtains would be drawn and I would be shut out and alone in the dark, all the while wishing I did belong.

How lonely to be on the outside looking in! Something as simple as watching happy families in church can intensify feelings of loss and isolation. These are the people who need our sensitive caring, compassion, and our faithful prayers. In calling people to compassion for the divorced, we are not excusing improper divorce or desertion. We simply need to suspend our judgments and care for those among us who are suffering.

Marriage is God's idea and ideal for us. He intended our lives to be woven together for better or for worse. We can rest assured that God shares our concern for troubled marriages. Whether our own or someone else's marriage, we should never give up simply because things *look* hopeless. Not only can God miraculously heal and restore marriages—He loves to!

Conclusion

God's weaving process is wonderful indeed. As we've seen, however, it is not without challenges and pain. We were designed to relate and to be woven into the fabric of other people's lives. While many can attest to the satisfaction (and occasional bliss) of this process, most of us would have to admit that being stretched, looped, and knotted can be uncomfortable and, at times, distressing.

Thankfully, as we travel the road to contentment in our relationships, we see fellow travelers who are successful. In their determination to "weave well," they are deeply committed to the steady nurturing and safeguarding that keep their relationships from unraveling. They would certainly admit it has not always been easy, but even through their trials, they probably would agree with Solomon, who said, "Two are better than one, because they have a good reward for their labor" (Eccles. 4:9).

These couples have discovered that God cannot lie. In seeking Him first, they have learned that His blueprint is best; His ideal is highest. Their commitment to be open and honest before God and each other has led them to trust their relationship to His truth and power. As a result, they experience fulfillment and happiness. Unlike so many relationships today, the love they enjoy is deeper than the skin and longer than the bed.

Through movies and television, Hollywood perpetuates the lie that life-long commitments are an outdated notion. A publisher of a pornographic magazine reportedly said that sex is simply a function of the body; a drive man shares with animals, like eating, drinking, and sleeping. Sex, he said, is a physiological demand that must be satisfied, or the resulting frustration will manifest itself in all kinds of neuroses and repressive psychoses. This pseudo-intellectual hogwash has undermined many marriages.

It is possible to have such a relationship. More than that, it is God's plan—a plan He gives us the power to accomplish. The

ratio of joy and satisfaction we experience will be in direct pro-
portion to our choice to listen to His voice and obediently follow the principles He has set forth.

There will always be questions about relationships simply
because it is our human nature to ask them. Every generation
ponders singleness, dating, marriage, and the like. Seminars,
conferences, books, and counseling sessions will, no doubt, continue to abound. Some will be worthwhile; others will be devoid
of anything good. In the midst of the myriad philosophies and
ideas about relationships, God's truth will still ring clearly
through His Word.

We each have a wonderful opportunity to make a difference
in this world. We can be living examples that our heavenly
"Father knows best." The God we serve is directly reflected in
our relationships.

In 1936, a radio broadcast was being transmitted from
England to America. Just before King Edward VIII was to
speak, someone stumbled over a wire in the control room of
WJZ (now WABC, New York) and snapped the only line of
communication between the two great countries. The engineers
were frantic. With only moments remaining before air time, a
quick-thinking apprentice grasped the two broken ends of wire,
allowing his body to literally bridge the gap. Seconds later, the
King addressed the nation, his words transmitted through the
body of that man. In a similar way, God's words can be transmitted through the people who love Him enough to follow His
commands and *demonstrate* His love.

It is in the demonstration of our love and commitment that
many of us experience weakness. An ambassador of the United
States was reassigned to Paris, France. In preparation, he
learned French and diligently studied about the country. As he
was leaving, a friend asked, "Ambassador, how is your
French?" He replied, "Oh, my French is excellent—all except
my verbs." Sounds like many Christians—our nouns are great:

Father, Lord, brother, friend; our adjectives are excellent: blessed, wonderful, holy; but our verbs: give, invite, serve, listen, love—they could use a little work.

Almost two thousand years ago, the first groups of Christians dotted the landscape of the Roman Empire. They held tenaciously to the truths that Jesus taught and the apostles passed down. The world tried to find fault and discrepancies in their words and actions. They couldn't. The Roman government began to feel threatened by this group of followers of Jesus Christ, so they sent spies into their congregations and churches to find out exactly what they were practicing and teaching.

One early historian wrote an account of a spy sent on such a mission to investigate a local assembly somewhere in the Roman Empire:

> These Christians are very strange people. They meet together in an empty room to worship. They don't have an image. They speak of one by the name of Jesus who is absent, but whom they seem to be expecting at any time. My, how they love Him and how they love one another.

Isn't that terrific? Life was boiled down to basics for that group, wasn't it? Their relationships with each other and with the Lord were the center of their fellowship. Wouldn't it be remarkable if a spy was sent to our churches today and came away saying:

> My, how they love their Lord! How they love their wives, husbands, and the members of their church. They show love and forgiveness in all their relationships and are content among themselves, yet they selflessly reach out to strangers. I want to be like them...I want to be a Christian.

This is how a separate life is woven into the fabric of another's. In the ultimate weaving, God draws us close and eternally connects us to Christ. This is God's love in action.

Perhaps the most famous and noteworthy treatise on love was penned by the Apostle Paul in 1 Corinthians—the same book that gives us so many principles for relationships:

> *Though I speak with the tongues of men and angels, but have not love, I have become sounding brass or a clanging cymbal. And though I have the gift of prophecy, and understand all mysteries and all knowledge, and though I have all faith, so that I could remove mountains, but have not love, I am nothing. And though I bestow all my goods to feed the poor, and though I have my body to be burned, but have not love, it profits me nothing. Love suffers long and is kind; love does not envy; love does not parade itself, is not puffed up; does not behave rudely, does not seek its own, is not provoked, thinks no evil; does not rejoice in iniquity, but rejoices in the truth; bears all things, believes all things, hopes all things, endures all things. Love never fails.... (1 Cor. 13:1-8a)*

This description of love epitomizes the life of Jesus Christ, doesn't it? Therefore, it follows that the more time we spend with Him, learning about Him, the more we will be able to love like Him.

Have you reached the end of your rope? Are you exhausted in your own efforts to "make it work"? Whether you are single, married, divorced, or remarried, the strength you need is found in Jesus Christ. You may have followed all the advice the world has to offer with no success. The difference between relationships that hang precariously by a thread and those that are woven together beautifully and securely is the unifying cord of God's presence, power, and love.